TEEN RIGHTS AND FREEDOMS

| Alcohol

Teen Rights and Freedoms

I Alcohol

Roman Espejo
Book Editor

GREENHAVEN PRESS
A part of Gale, Cengage Learning

Detroit • New York • San Francisco • New Haven, Conn • Waterville, Maine • London

Elizabeth Des Chenes, *Director, Publishing Solutions*

For more information, contact:
Greenhaven Press
27500 Drake Rd.
Farmington Hills, MI 48331-3535
Or you can visit our Internet site at gale.cengage.com.

For product information and technology assistance, contact us at:

Gale Customer Support, 1-800-877-4253.
For permission to use material from this text or product, submit all requests online at www.cengage.com/permissions.

Further permissions questions can be emailed to permissionrequest@cengage.com.

Articles in Greenhaven Press anthologies are often edited for length to meet page requirements. In addition, original titles of these works are changed to clearly present the main thesis and to explicitly indicate the author's opinion. Every effort is made to ensure the Greenhaven Press accurately reflects the original intent of the authors. Every effort has been made to trace the owners of copyrighted material.

Cover Image © Stokkete/Shutterstock.com.

LIBRARY OF CONGRESS CATALOGING-IN-PUBLICATION DATA

Alcohol / Roman Espejo, Book Editor.
    p. cm. -- (Teen rights and freedoms)
    Includes bibliographical references and index.
    ISBN 978-0-7377-6398-0 (hbk.)
 1. Youth--Alcohol use--United States. 2. Drinking age--Law and legislation--United States. 3. Drinking of alcoholic beverages--United States. 4. Liquor laws--United States. I. Espejo, Roman, 1977- editor of compilation.
    HV5135.A385843 2013
    362.2920835'0973--dc23

                                                                    2012032615

Printed in the United States of America
1 2 3 4 5 6 7 16 15 14 13 12

Contents

1. ## The National Minimum Drinking Age Act
   ## Is Constitutional   11
   ### The Supreme Court's Decision

   William Rehnquist

   A US Supreme Court Justice contends that the law to
   withhold federal highway funds from states that do not
   raise their minimum drinking age to twenty-one protects public safety and only imposes a small penalty for
   noncompliance.

2. ## The National Minimum Drinking Age Act
   ## Violates Youths' and States' Rights   20

   Alex Koroknay-Palicz

   The executive director of a youth rights organization
   claims that the policy of withholding federal highway
   funds to raise the minimum drinking age "blackmailed"
   states to change their alcohol laws and was based on distorted drunk-driving statistics.

3. ## The Minimum Drinking Age of Twenty-One
   ## Is Justified   31
   ### The Louisiana Supreme Court's Decision

   Jeffrey P. Victory

   An associate justice for the Louisiana Supreme Court
   contends that outlawing the sale of alcohol to eighteen-

to twenty-year-olds is not discriminatory based on the high proportion of drivers in that age group involved in drunk-driving accidents.

and commercial availability of alcohol to minors under tighter control.

Citing a variety of constitutional infringements that may occur with alcohol screening at school dances, an attorney advises that schools considering the policy must ensure that it protects the civil rights of students.

Foreword

*"In the truest sense freedom cannot be
bestowed, it must be achieved."*
Franklin D. Roosevelt,
September 16, 1936

The notion of children and teens having rights is a relatively recent development. Early in American history, the head of the household—nearly always the father—exercised complete control over the children in the family. Children were legally considered to be the property of their parents. Over time, this view changed, as society began to acknowledge that children have rights independent of their parents, and that the law should protect young people from exploitation. By the early twentieth century, more and more social reformers focused on the welfare of children, and over the ensuing decades advocates worked to protect them from harm in the workplace, to secure public education for all, and to guarantee fair treatment for youths in the criminal justice system. Throughout the twentieth century, rights for children and teens—and restrictions on those rights—were established by Congress and reinforced by the courts. Today's courts are still defining and clarifying the rights and freedoms of young people, sometimes expanding those rights and sometimes limiting them. Some teen rights are outside the scope of public law and remain in the realm of the family, while still others are determined by school policies.

Each volume in the Teen Rights and Freedoms series focuses on a different right or freedom and offers an anthology of key essays and articles on that right or freedom and the responsibilities that come with it. Material within each volume is drawn from a diverse selection of primary and secondary sources—journals, magazines, newspapers, nonfiction books, organization newsletters, position papers, speeches, and government documents, with a particular emphasis on Supreme Court and lower court decisions. Volumes also include first-person narratives from young people and others involved in teen rights issues, such as parents and educators. The material is selected and arranged to highlight all the major social and legal controversies relating to the right or freedom under discussion. Each selection is preceded by an introduction that provides context and background. In many cases, the essays point to the difference between adult and teen rights, and why this difference exists.

Many of the volumes cover rights guaranteed under the Bill of Rights and how these rights are interpreted and protected in regard to children and teens, including freedom of speech, freedom of the press, due process, and religious rights. The scope of the series also encompasses rights or freedoms, whether real or perceived, relating to the school environment, such as electronic devices, dress, Internet policies, and privacy. Some volumes focus on the home environment, including topics such as parental control and sexuality.

Numerous features are included in each volume of Teen Rights and Freedoms:

- An annotated **table of contents** provides a brief summary of each essay in the volume and highlights court decisions and personal narratives.

- An **introduction** specific to the volume topic gives context for the right or freedom and its impact on daily life.

- A brief **chronology** offers important dates associated with the right or freedom, including landmark court cases.

- **Primary sources**—including personal narratives and court decisions—are among the varied selections in the anthology.

- **Illustrations**—including photographs, charts, graphs, tables, statistics, and maps—are closely tied to the text and chosen to help readers understand key points or concepts.

- An annotated list of **organizations to contact** presents sources of additional information on the topic.
- A **for further reading** section offers a bibliography of books, periodical articles, and Internet sources for further research.
- A comprehensive subject **index** provides access to key people, places, events, and subjects cited in the text.

Each volume of Teen Rights and Freedoms delves deeply into the issues most relevant to the lives of teens: their own rights, freedoms, and responsibilities. With the help of this series, students and other readers can explore from many angles the evolution and current expression of rights both historic and contemporary.

Introduction

For US youth, turning twenty-one—the minimum drinking age—is regarded as a civil and cultural milestone in the transition to adulthood. What many teens may not know is that this drinking age has only been in effect since 1984, when the US Congress passed the National Minimum Drinking Age Act, and was not established in all states until 1988. Under the act, the minimum drinking age was still left up to the states; those that did not comply would be subject to a ten-percent reduction of federal highway funds. Contrary to widespread perceptions, drinking is not outright banned for persons under twenty-one; it is their purchase and possession of alcohol that is illegal. Only Alabama, Idaho, Indiana, Kansas, North Carolina, Pennsylvania, Vermont, and the District of Columbia ban all alcohol consumption for those under the minimum drinking age. Twenty states have no consumption restrictions based on age, and the remaining have partial age restrictions, making exceptions for a variety of situations—from drinking with guardian consent to imbibing wine for religious purposes. Before 1984, some states had minimum drinking ages as low as eighteen or nineteen years of age. In the 1960s and 1970s, amid the Vietnam War and enactment of the Twenty-Sixth Amendment—which set the voting age at eighteen—twenty-nine states lowered their drinking ages under twenty-one. The momentum later reversed with reports indicating that alcohol-related traffic deaths among teen drivers were increasing and with the founding of Mothers Against Drunk Driving (MADD) in 1980.

But the minimum drinking age and alcohol consumption by youths under twenty-one persisted as a contentious rights issue, as evidenced by key lawsuits in the nation's courts. *South Dakota v. Dole* (1987), a case heard by the US Supreme Court, challenged the constitutionality of the National Minimum Drinking Age Act. In delivering the court's opinion, Chief Justice William

Rehnquist defended it as constitutional. "Even if Congress might lack the power to impose a national minimum drinking age directly, we conclude that encouragement to state action found in [the act] is a valid use of the spending power," he stated. In dissent, Justice Sandra Day O'Connor opposed the decision. "It is an attempt to regulate the sale of liquor, an attempt that lies outside Congress' power to regulate commerce because it falls within . . . the Twenty-First Amendment," she argued, referring to the constitutional amendment that ended Prohibition in 1933. The minimum drinking age and discrimination against youth was examined in *Manuel v. State* (1996), wherein numerous individuals and retailers sued the state of Louisiana for its compliance with the National Minimum Drinking Age Act. The trial court ruled that prohibiting the sale of alcohol to eighteen- to twenty-year-olds was discriminatory, which was initially upheld—then reversed—by the Louisiana Supreme Court. On rehearing, it cited the age group's excessive involvement in drunk-driving accidents.

Other court cases have focused on the liabilities of underage drinking. The legal responsibility of social hosts who furnish alcoholic beverages to minors was decided in *Wakulich v. Mraz* (2003), which reached the Illinois Supreme Court. In June 1997, sixteen-year-old Elizabeth Wakulich finished a quart of Goldschlager liquor provided by brothers Michael and Brian Mraz, who bet her $80 to do it. When Wakulich became unconscious and noticeably ill, the Mrazs did not seek treatment for her and prevented others from calling for assistance. The teen died from alcohol poisoning. The Wakulichs filed a suit against the Mrazs, bringing allegations of negligence and enabling underage drinking. Still, the court found that state law exempts social hosts from liability in serving alcohol, arguing that the law would be applied too broadly if such exemptions were not in place. *Bell v. Hutsell* (2011), another Illinois Supreme Court case, determined the accountability of parents who allow their children to drink or have parties with liquor. In October 2006, eighteen-year-old high school graduate Daniel Bell crashed his car into a tree after drinking at the family home of fellow graduate Jonathan Hutsell, fatally injuring himself and one of his four passengers. The Bells sued the Hutsells for negligence—for failing to fulfill their spoken intention to prevent underage drinking at the party. But the court ruled that the Hutsells had not acted affirmatively to establish what is known as a voluntary undertaking—in this instance, confiscating alcohol from anyone underage or ending the party. Because the Hutsells did not actively undertake a duty to protect their guests, they were not found guilty of violating that duty and were not held liable for Bell's death.

Binge drinking at colleges and universities across the country has also brought attention to underage alcohol consumption. The National Institute on Alcohol Abuse and Alcoholism defines binge drinking as five drinks for men or four drinks for women over the course of two hours, when the blood alcohol concentration (BAC) level reaches 0.08 or higher. At this level, there are slight impairments to speech, vision, hearing, and reaction times, with greater impairment to memory and reasoning. According to a March 15, 2012, story on NPR.org, approximately 44 percent of college students binge drink. And a March 2012 study published in *Health Affairs*, which tracked 986 students at five schools, reported that half of the students blacked out from alcohol use at least once in the past year. The prevalence of college binge drinking has caused alarm among many college administrators. Some have suggested a loosening of restrictions rather than stricter enforcement; thus binge drinking statistics have actually given rise to a movement to lower the drinking age. John McCardell, president emeritus of Middlebury College in Vermont, created Choose Responsibility in 2007, a nonprofit organization asserting that the current law encourages clandestine drinking, leading to bingeing and other harmful consumption behaviors among the underaged. The organization recommends that an education-based, graduated alcohol licensing system for eighteen- to twenty-year-olds take its place. A year later,

Choose Responsibility launched the Amethyst Initiative, which has gained the signed endorsement of 136 college presidents and chancellors for a reevaluation of the National Minimum Drinking Age Act. But not all university heads support the initiative. "I remember college campuses when we had 18-year-old drinking ages, and I honestly believe we've made some progress," Donna Shalala, University of Miami president and former US Secretary of Health and Human Services, tells CBS News. "To just shift it back down to the high schools makes no sense at all."

The debate over the complexity of alcohol regulations and restrictions continues to unfold in the United States. *Teen Rights and Freedoms: Alcohol* examines the minimum drinking age and its impact on society.

Chronology

October 28, 1919   The National Prohibition Act, also known as the Volstead Act, is enacted, prohibiting alcoholic beverages and regulating the manufacture, sale, and transport of alcohol.

January 17, 1920   The Eighteenth Amendment to the Constitution goes into effect, starting the Prohibition era in the United States.

December 5, 1933   The Twenty-First Amendment is ratified, thereby ending the Prohibition era. It allows states to set their own alcohol laws.

July 1, 1971   The Twenty-Sixth Amendment is adopted, lowering the voting age from twenty-one to eighteen years old. The amendment influences many states to also lower their minimum drinking ages.

May 7, 1980   Candy Lightner forms the nonprofit organization Mothers Against Drunk Driving (MADD) after her thirteen-year-old daughter Cari is killed by an intoxicated driver in California.

May 8, 1982   In Minnesota, officials at Truman High School use breathalyzer testing to screen students who appear drunk at its junior-senior prom.

July 17, 1984   The National Minimum Drinking Age
Act is passed, requiring all states to enforce a minimum legal drinking age of
twenty-one or lose 10 percent of federal
highway funds.

August 6, 1986   The Massachusetts Supreme Judicial
Court decides in *McGuiggan v. New
England Telephone & Telegraph Co.*
that a social host providing alcohol
"to an adult guest may be liable for a
death caused shortly thereafter by that
guest's negligent operation of a motor
vehicle while under the influence of
alcohol."

June 23, 1987   In *South Dakota v. Dole*, the US
Supreme Court rules that the partial
withdrawal of federal highway funds
from states not complying with the
National Minimum Drinking Age Act
is constitutional.

March 8, 1996   On rehearing a case decided previously, the Louisiana Supreme Court
decides in *Manuel v. State* that banning the sale of alcohol to individuals
between eighteen and twenty-one years
old is not discriminatory, citing the age
group's disproportionate involvement in
alcohol-related car accidents.

1998   The National Youth Rights Association
(NYRA) is established to advocate the
civil liberties of minors. Lowering the

minimum legal drinking age of twenty-
one is a major part of NYRA's platform.

February 6, 2003

The Illinois Supreme Court issues its
opinion in *Wakulich v. Mraz*, upholding
that social hosts are not liable for serving alcohol to guests, whether adults or
minors, because such a law would be
applied too liberally.

July 2008

A group of college and university
professors and chancellors forms the
Amethyst Initiative, which advocates a
reevaluation of the minimum drinking
age in the United States. The initiative
claims that the drinking age of twenty-
one encourages binge drinking and the
clandestine consumption of alcohol
among youth.

July 15, 2009

In Richland County, South Carolina,
Magistrate Mel Maurer declares that
state laws prohibiting the possession and consumption of alcohol by
eighteen- to twenty-year-olds infringe
upon South Carolina's constitution. A
week later, Chief Magistrate of Aiken
County Roger Edmonds hands down
the same decision.

May 19, 2011

In *Bell v. Hutsell*, the Illinois Appellate
Court maintains that adults who permit
underage drinking on their property
are not liable if they do not affirmatively
establish a voluntary undertaking.

> *"We find this legislative effort within constitutional bounds even if Congress may not regulate drinking ages directly."*

The National Minimum Drinking Age Act Is Constitutional

The Supreme Court's Decision

William Rehnquist

The National Minimum Drinking Age Act of 1984 raised the minimum drinking age to twenty-one through the withholding of federal highway funds from states with lower drinking ages. South Dakota, which permitted nineteen-year-olds to purchase beer, challenged the law's constitutionality in South Dakota v. Dole. *In the following viewpoint, Justice William Rehnquist argues that the US Congress may attach conditions to federal funds under certain restrictions and to serve the general welfare. Rehnquist insists that the law increases traffic safety by preventing youth from driving to other states with lower drinking ages to consume alcohol. Furthermore, the law is not coercive, as it would withhold only a small percentage of federal funds, he maintains. Rehnquist was*

William Rehnquist, Majority opinion, *South Dakota v. Dole*, US Supreme Court, June 23, 1987.

the sixteenth chief justice of the United States, serving in the US Supreme Court from 1972 to 2005.

Petitioner South Dakota permits persons 19 years of age or older to purchase beer containing up to 3.2% alcohol. S. D. Codified Laws 35-6-27. In 1984 Congress enacted 23 U.S.C. 158 which directs the Secretary of Transportation to withhold a percentage of federal highway funds otherwise allocable from States "in which the purchase or public possession . . . of any alcoholic beverage by a person who is less than twenty-one years of age is lawful." The State sued in United States District Court seeking a declaratory judgment that 158 violates the constitutional limitations on congressional exercise of the spending power and violates the Twenty-first Amendment[1] to the United States Constitution. The District Court rejected the State's claims, and the Court of Appeals for the Eighth Circuit affirmed.

In this Court, the parties direct most of their efforts to defining the proper scope of the Twenty-first Amendment. Relying on our statement in *California Retail Liquor Dealers Assn. v. Midcal Aluminum, Inc.*, that the "Twenty-first Amendment grants the States virtually complete control over whether to permit importation or sale of liquor and how to structure the liquor distribution system," South Dakota asserts that the setting of minimum drinking ages is clearly within the "core powers" reserved to the States under [section] 2 of the Amendment. Brief for Petitioner, petitioner claims, usurps that core power. The Secretary in response asserts that the Twenty-first Amendment is simply not implicated by 158; the plain language of 2 confirms the States' broad power to impose restrictions on the sale and distribution of alcoholic beverages but does not confer on them any power to permit sales that Congress seeks to prohibit. That Amendment, under this reasoning, would not prevent Congress from affirmatively enacting a national minimum drinking age more restrictive than that provided by the vari-

US president Ronald Reagan signs the National Minimum Drinking Age Act of 1984. Among those in attendance is Candy Lightner (second from left), the founder of Mothers Against Drunk Driving (MADD). © Bettmann/Corbis.

ous state laws; and it would follow a fortiori that the indirect inducement involved here is compatible with the Twenty-first Amendment.

These arguments present questions of the meaning of the Twenty-first Amendment, the bounds of which have escaped precise definition. Despite the extended treatment of the question by the parties, however, we need not decide in this case whether that Amendment would prohibit an attempt by

Congress to legislate directly a national minimum drinking age. Here, Congress has acted indirectly under its spending power to encourage uniformity in the States' drinking ages. As we explain below, we find this legislative effort within constitutional bounds even if Congress may not regulate drinking ages directly.

The Constitution empowers Congress to "lay and collect Taxes, Duties, Imposts, and Excises, to pay the Debts and provide for the common Defence and general Welfare of the United States." Incident to this power, Congress may attach conditions on the receipt of federal funds, and has repeatedly employed the power "to further broad policy objectives by conditioning receipt of federal moneys upon compliance by the recipient with federal statutory and administrative directives." The breadth of this power was made clear in *United States v. Butler*, where the Court, resolving a longstanding debate over the scope of the Spending Clause, determined that "the power of Congress to authorize expenditure of public moneys for public purposes is not limited by the direct grants of legislative power found in the Constitution." Thus, objectives not thought to be within Article I's "enumerated legislative fields," may nevertheless be attained through the use of the spending power and the conditional grant of federal funds.

Consistent with the Restrictions

The spending power is of course not unlimited, but is instead subject to several general restrictions articulated in our cases. The first of these limitations is derived from the language of the Constitution itself: the exercise of the spending power must be in pursuit of "the general welfare." In considering whether a particular expenditure is intended to serve general public purposes, courts should defer substantially to the judgment of Congress. Second, we have required that if Congress desires to condition the States' receipt of federal funds, it "must do so unambiguously . . . , enabl[ing] the States to exercise their choice knowingly, cognizant of the consequences of their participation." Third, our cases have suggested (without significant elaboration) that conditions on federal grants might be illegitimate if they are unrelated "to the federal interest in particular national projects or programs."

Finally, we have noted that other constitutional provisions may provide an independent bar to the conditional grant of federal funds.

South Dakota does not seriously claim that 158 is inconsistent with any of the first three restrictions mentioned above. We can readily conclude that the provision is designed to serve the general welfare, especially in light of the fact that "the concept of welfare or the opposite is shaped by Congress. . . ." Congress found that the differing drinking ages in the States created particular incentives for young persons to combine their desire to drink with their ability to drive, and that this interstate problem required a national solution. The means it chose to address this dangerous situation were reasonably calculated to advance the general welfare. The conditions upon which States receive the funds, moreover, could not be more clearly stated by Congress. And the State itself, rather than challenging the germaneness of the condition to federal purposes, admits that it "has never contended that the congressional action was . . . unrelated to a national concern in the absence of the Twenty-first Amendment." Indeed, the condition imposed by Congress is directly related to one of the main purposes for which highway funds are expended—safe interstate travel. This goal of the interstate highway system had been frustrated by varying drinking ages among the States. A Presidential commission appointed to study alcohol-related accidents and fatalities on the Nation's highways concluded that the lack of uniformity in the States' drinking ages created "an incentive to drink and drive" because "young persons commut[e] to border States where the drinking age is lower." By enacting 158, Congress conditioned the receipt of federal funds in a way reasonably calculated to address

Public Possession of Alcohol and Minors

The national law specifically requires states to prohibit purchase and public possession of alcoholic beverages. It does not require prohibition of persons under 21 (also called youth or minors) from drinking alcoholic beverages. The term "public possession" is strictly defined and does not apply to possession for the following:

- An established religious purpose, when accompanied by a parent, spouse, or legal guardian age 21 or older;
- Medical purposes when prescribed or administered by a licensed physician, pharmacist, dentist, nurse, hospital, or medical institution;
- In private clubs or establishments; and
- In the course of lawful employment by a duly licensed manufacturer, wholesaler or retailer.

Pam Beer and Trina Leonard, Community How-To Guide on Public Policy Underage Drinking Prevention Project. *Collington, PA: Diane Publishing Company, 2001.*

this particular impediment to a purpose for which the funds are expended.

The Twenty-First Amendment and Drinking Ages

The remaining question about the validity of 158—and the basic point of disagreement between the parties—is whether the Twenty-first Amendment constitutes an "independent constitutional bar" to the conditional grant of federal funds. Petitioner, relying on its view that the Twenty-first Amendment prohibits direct regulation of drinking ages by Congress, asserts that "Congress may not use the spending power to regulate that which it is prohibited from regulating directly under the Twenty-first Amendment." But our cases show that this "independent constitutional bar" limitation on the spending power is not of the kind petitioner suggests. *United States v. Butler*, for example, established that the constitutional limitations on Congress when exercising its spending power are less exacting than those on its authority to regulate directly.

We have also held that a perceived Tenth Amendment limitation on congressional regulation of state affairs did not concomitantly limit the range of conditions legitimately placed on federal grants. In *Oklahoma v. Civil Service Comm'n*, the Court considered the validity of the Hatch Act[2] insofar as it was applied to political activities of state officials whose employment was financed in whole or in part with federal funds. The State contended that an order under this provision to withhold certain federal funds unless a state official was removed invaded its sovereignty in violation of the Tenth Amendment. Though finding that "the United States is not concerned with, and has no power to regulate, local political activities as such of state officials," the Court nevertheless held that the Federal Government "does have power to fix the terms upon which its money allotments to states shall be disbursed." The Court found no violation of the State's sovereignty because the State could, and did, adopt "the 'simple expedient' of not yielding to what she urges is federal coercion. The offer of benefits to a state by the United States dependent upon cooperation by the state with federal plans, assumedly for the general welfare, is not unusual."

These cases establish that the "independent constitutional bar" limitation on the spending power is not, as petitioner suggests, a prohibition on the indirect achievement of objectives which Congress is not empowered to achieve directly. Instead, we think that the language in our earlier opinions stands for the unexceptionable proposition that the power may not be used to induce the States to engage in activities that would themselves be unconstitutional. Thus, for example, a grant of federal funds conditioned on invidiously discriminatory state action or the infliction of cruel and unusual punishment would be an illegitimate exercise of the Congress' broad spending power. But no such claim can be or is made here. Were South Dakota to succumb to the blandishments offered by Congress and raise its drinking age to 21, the State's action in so doing would not violate the constitutional rights of anyone.

Mild, Not Coercive, Encouragement

Our decisions have recognized that in some circumstances the financial inducement offered by Congress might be so coercive as to pass the point at which "pressure turns into compulsion." Here, however, Congress has directed only that a State desiring to establish a minimum drinking age lower than 21 lose a relatively small percentage of certain federal highway funds. Petitioner contends that the coercive nature of this program is evident from the degree of success it has achieved. We cannot conclude, however, that a conditional grant of federal money of this sort is unconstitutional simply by reason of its success in achieving the congressional objective.

When we consider, for a moment, that all South Dakota would lose if she adheres to her chosen course as to a suitable minimum drinking age is 5% of the funds otherwise obtainable under specified highway grant programs, the argument as to coercion is shown to be more rhetoric than fact. As we said a half century ago in *Steward Machine Co. v. Davis*:

> [E]very rebate from a tax when conditioned upon conduct is in some measure a temptation. But to hold that motive or temptation is equivalent to coercion is to plunge the law in endless difficulties. The outcome of such a doctrine is the acceptance of a philosophical determinism by which choice becomes impossible. [Until] now the law has been guided by a robust common sense which assumes the freedom of the will as a working hypothesis in the solution of its problems.

Here Congress has offered relatively mild encouragement to the States to enact higher minimum drinking ages than they would otherwise choose. But the enactment of such laws remains the prerogative of the States not merely in theory but in fact. Even if Congress might lack the power to impose a national minimum drinking age directly, we conclude that encouragement to state action found in 158 is a valid use of the spending power. Accordingly, the judgment of the Court of Appeals is affirmed.

Notes

1. The Twenty-first Amendment to the US Constitution repealed the Eighteenth Amendment, thus ending the national ban on the sale, manufacture and transport of alcohol
2. The Hatch Act, signed into law in 1939, prohibits partisan political activities by employees of the US government's executive branch with the exception of the President, Vice President, and certain other high-level officials.

> "The National Minimum Drinking Age
> was a key defeat, both for states' rights
> and for youth rights."

The National Minimum Drinking Age Act Violates Youths' and States' Rights

Alex Koroknay-Palicz

In the following viewpoint, Alex Koroknay-Palicz argues that the National Minimum Drinking Age Act is an affront to the rights of youths and states. Signed into law in 1984, the minimum drinking age of twenty-one is relatively recent, backed by special interest groups and politicians seeking publicity and votes, he contends. Many states had legalized drinking for those under twenty-one, but Koroknay-Palicz maintains that the National Minimum Drinking Age Act "blackmailed" them into raising their minimum drinking ages with threats of withholding federal highway funds. He insists exaggerated statistics on youths and drunken driving also influenced public opinion and the congressional enactment of the raised drinking age. Koroknay-Palicz served as executive director of the National Youth Rights Association until 2011.

The National Minimum Drinking Age Act is perhaps the law that has the most impact on the day-to-day lives of America's youth since it was signed into law on July 17, 1984. While the 21-year-old drinking age seems imbedded in American society, it is only a recent innovation. Most people do not know that the drinking age was only made a national law in 1984, and only after a determined battle by special interest groups.

The History of the Act

The history of the National Minimum Drinking Age Act truly started back before Prohibition. The temperance movement used selective prohibition (drinking ages) as a stepping-stone approach to their goal of out-lawing all alcohol. Finally they did achieve the goal of total prohibition of alcohol, when in 1919 the 18th Amendment to the Constitution was ratified. Due to the obvious ineffectiveness of Prohibition and the change in public opinion, the 18th Amendment was repealed in 1933 by the 21st Amendment. What followed was a compromise with the lingering temperance movement and the modern drinking age was established. [Sociologist and author Mike A. Males states:] "The political failure of general Prohibition meant that American adults would increasingly focus justifications for alcohol policy less on the perils of drunkenness and more on the tenuous concept that adults can drink properly but youths cannot or should not."

From the end of Prohibition until 1984, drinking ages were determined by the states—many of them had the age at 21 while several lowered the age to 18 for the purchase of beer. This was changed by the activism of the "Baby Boom" generation during the Vietnam War. [Males explains,] "From 1970 through 1975 nearly all states lowered their legal ages of adulthood, thirty including their legal drinking ages, usually from 21 to 18." It was argued that if people were required to fight and die in a foreign war then they should be allowed the privilege of drinking alcohol. This generation exercised previously unheard-of clout and

BEFORE THERE WAS A NATIONAL DRINKING AGE

Minimum legal drinking age by state in 1984

- Age 18 (7 states and DC)
- Age 19 (17 states)
- Age 20 (4 states)
- Age 21 (22 states)

*Age for beer and wine only; twenty-one for hard liquor.

Taken from: *Chicago Tribune*/Congressional Research Service.

political muscle, and through years of protest and many valid arguments this generation of youth gained back some lost liberty. After this period, however, public sentiment changed. The baby boomers were aging and the freedoms they fought to secure for themselves no longer seemed important when they involved someone else.

The Movement Led by Mothers Against Drunk Driving

This loss of a powerful ally allowed the modern prohibitionist movement led by Candy Lightner, the president and founder of

Mothers Against Drunk Driving (MADD), to gain strength in this country again. The late seventies and eighties were marked with an excess of highly publicized studies that claimed teenage alcohol use was out of control and turning into a devastating problem of epidemic proportions. This and the national mood produced an environment primed for the anti-alcohol, anti-youth legislation that became the National Minimum Drinking Age Act of 1984.

The actual bill required [according to the *Thomas Senate Record Vote Analysis*] "all States to raise their minimum drinking age to 21 within 2 years or lose a portion of their Federal-aid highway funds; and encourage States, through incentive grants programs, to pass mandatory sentencing laws to combat drunk driving." The portion of the Federal-aid highway funds that would be lost if a state didn't comply amounted to 5 percent in the third year and 10 percent in the fourth year.

This bill was created and acted upon by many dynamic people. Certainly the person who had the most impact upon this legislation was Candy Lightner, who founded the organization MADD after a drunk driver killed her daughter in 1980. After that traumatic event Lightner turned her grief into revenge and founded the powerful lobbying organization that claimed a membership of three-hundred thousand in 44 states by 1984. Another highly visible character in the story was the President of the United States, Ronald Reagan. Reagan had initially threatened to veto the bill, citing the provisions to punish states for non-compliance as an infringement upon states' rights. Reagan later changed from opposition to support, formally announcing this on June 13, 1984.

Many congressmen were involved in the long process that created this piece of legislation. Frank R. Lautenberg (D-N.J.) was the senator who proposed the senate amendment to house bill H.R. 4616. This amendment was the "first piece of legislation he has successfully sponsored since his election in 1982" [according to Steven Gettinger]. Sen. Gordon Humphrey (R-N.H.)

proposed an opposing amendment to Lautenberg's, one that offered benefits to states that complied rather than penalties to those that didn't. Opposition was further led by Sen. Steven D. Symms (R-Idaho). Rep. James J. Howard (D-N.J.), Chairman of the Public Works and Transportation Committee, got the Senate amendment onto the House calendar before the upcoming recess. Rep. Howard was also the person who had "offered the legislation that set a nationwide speed limit of 55 m.p.h" [according to Jane Perlez]. Rep. Glenn M. Anderson (D-Calif.) proposed H.R. 4616 that later became the vehicle for the drinking age amendment. Sen. Lowell P. Weicker Jr. (R-Conn.) held up Senate action because he felt that raising the drinking age wasn't doing enough for the problem of drunk driving as a whole.

The drinking age legislation can be primarily attributed to the efforts of Candy Lightner and the MADD organization. After its founding, MADD set out on a massive campaign to raise the drinking age on a state-by-state basis, and then finally on a national level. Lightner's national campaign started when she "buttonholed congressmen while representatives of MADD chapters flooded their offices with letters and telegrams" [according to Gettinger]. She gained the support of New Jersey Rep. Howard, who proposed an amendment to the transportation bill, H.R. 5504. H.R. 5504 involved the allocation for funds for highway and road projects around the country. There was much controversy surrounding this bill due to the multitude of pet projects that were added on. A total of $575 million extra was added onto H.R. 5504, but was eventually cut back to $106 million. On June 7, 1984 the House voted 297-73 in favor of the amended highway bill. The Senate drafted a similar bill (S 2527), which [Gettinger explains] became "mired in a controversy of its own and has not come to the floor." Sen. Lautenberg, who proposed the drinking age provision, chose then to add it to H.R. 4616 instead of H.R. 5504.

However, Lautenberg was blocked from bringing his amendment to the floor by Sen. Weicker, who had [Gettinger explains] "held up Senate action because he wanted a broader approach than the focus on the minimum drinking age." A compromise was reached and other provisions regarding adult drunk driving were added to the amendment.

Heated Discussions

The most passionate and heated discussion over the drinking age amendment occurred here on the Senate floor. Several conservatives fought Lautenberg's attempt to blackmail the states into following the national government. Led by Sen. Humphrey and Sen. Symms, the opposition proposed an amendment to counter Lautenberg's amendment. Humphrey's amendment offered positive incentives to states that complied rather than threatening them with penalties such as loss of significant funding. Lautenberg's opponents considered his amendment to be an infringement on state's rights; their arguments, made on June 26, taken from *Thomas Senate [Record] Vote Analysis*, are as follows:

> The pending Lautenberg amendment, however, which would coerce States into establishing a 21-year-old drinking age, should be rejected because it would result in Federal encroachment into areas that have been reserved to the States under the Constitution. It is clear that all powers not specifically delegated to the Federal Government by the Constitution are reserved to the States and to the people. Nowhere in the Constitution has the power to regulate the sale and consumption of alcoholic beverages been delegated to the Federal Government. Those who want to expand the power of the Federal Government beyond that granted to it by the Constitution have found various mechanisms for achieving their objective. Almost every Federal tax dollar returned to the States has strings attached; the Lautenberg amendment would tighten the knot. This practice, as embodied by this amendment, is nothing short of blackmail by the Federal Government. It is inconsistent with the Constitution, contrary to sound principles of federalism,

and not in the best interest of our country. Therefore, the Lautenberg amendment should be rejected.

In addition to the states' rights arguments, opponents to the legislation maintained that any attempt to deny someone the right to drink alcohol was age discrimination. "Why the magic age of 21?" asked Sen. Patrick J. Leahy (D-Vt.). "Why not 25? How about 30, 35, 40?"

Enveloping Congress and the Country

In the end, however these arguments fell on deaf ears. Supporters of the Lautenberg amendment accused the Humphrey amendment of taking "half measures." The Humphrey amendment lost by a margin of 35-62, and the Lautenberg amendment passed by a margin of 81-16. The votes were largely non-partisan, although there was more Republican support for the Humphrey amendment. The breakdowns, taken from Republican Policy Committee's *Senate Record Vote Analysis,* are as follows:

On the Lautenberg amendment:

	YEA	NAY
Republicans	(45 or 82%)	(10 or 18%)
Democrats	(36 or 86%)	(6 or 14%)

On the Humphrey amendment:

	YEA	NAY
Republicans	(25 or 45%)	(30 or 55%)
Democrats	(10 or 24%)	(32 or 76%)

The non-partisan approval of this legislation can be most accurately described by this knowledgeable Senate source [quoted in the *Washington Post*], "The 21-year-old minimum drinking age is now seen as good public policy, one you can't lose on, and this is an election year." The mass hysteria over this issue so enveloped the congress and the country that even the President, who had previously condemned this amendment for being an infringement on states' rights, reversed his stance and on June 13 formally endorsed raising the drinking age. After Senate approval of Lautenberg's amendment it was sent back to the House where it silently passed through with no objections to the Senate version of the bill. This action made the drinking age public law on June 28, 1984. It seems that most of the leaders of the drinking age idea were from New Jersey, from Lautenberg in the Senate to Howard in the House. Not long before this issue was introduced in Washington, New Jersey had just raised their drinking age to 21, so the idea may have been very politically popular in the state of its originators.

The Media's Role

The media played an important role in this too, much overhyping the statistics and studies, which inflamed public opinion on the issue and no doubt affected the votes of more than a few congressmen. The statistics used in this public relations battle had several problems as well. For example, one set of statistics that was used in the debate on the Senate floor in favor of the Lautenberg amendment was as follows:

> Young drivers are involved in one of every five fatal auto accidents. Almost 60 percent of fatally injured teenagers were found to have alcohol in their blood; 43 percent of those were legally intoxicated. Five thousand of those killed on our highways each year are teenagers—a fifth of all auto fatalities—although teenagers account for only 10 percent of all drivers and travel only 9 percent of all miles driven.

These statistics, taken from *Thomas Senate Vote Analysis*, said that 5,000 killed on our highways are teenagers, one fifth of the total fatalities, which would mean the total is 25,000. It says that 43 percent of those 5,000 teenagers, or 2,150, were legally

University of Kansas students participate in a protest in 2004 aimed at lowering the drinking age to eighteen. Some critics of the National Minimum Drinking Age Act argue that it isn't logical to have different minimum ages for alcohol consumption and military service. © AP Images.

intoxicated (5,000 × .43 = 2,150). So 2,150 drunk teens out of 25,000 total accidents—that is 8 percent, not 20 percent as they imply. It is unknown how many were actually driving. Some of those 2,150 could have been sitting in the back seat while their parents were driving. Drinking age proponents such as MADD used statistics like these to obscure the truth in order to win their goal of further depriving youth of their liberty.

Blackmailing the States

Personally I agree with what the Humphrey supporters had to say—that the minimum drinking age is discriminatory based on age, and that it goes against the constitution by forcing the states to comply with the federal government. This legislation was disastrous for the concept of federalism, because it was one of the first steps that allowed the federal government to "blackmail" the states in this way. After the precedent was set by the National Minimum Drinking Age Act, coercive deals like this became common legislation on the hill.

Information on the House side of the story is difficult to find. It seems that the House amendments were not voted on individually, as were the Senate amendments. The sources that I found were very unclear about the process of moving the drinking age amendment from H.R. 5504 to H.R. 4616. Reporting of committee testimony seemed to favor the amendment as well. Every source mentioned MADD, but only one seems to have mentioned that student groups and restaurant owners came to testify against the bill. The opposing side of the issue was nearly non-existent in the newspapers. Only *CQ Weekly* mentioned the arguments for the anti-drinking age side in any detail.

Conclusions about the legislative process are not cheery ones. It seems to me that politicians are too eager to jump on band-wagons that promise good publicity and easy votes. It also seems to me that special interest groups such as MADD can exert tremendous influence upon legislation and the public mood on an issue. It was interesting that such a fiery debate raged in the Senate, but when it went back to the House it was passed through with less than a murmur. President Reagan also had an interesting role. His declarations of support and opposition helped shape public opinion and helped motivate congressmen in his party.

The National Minimum Drinking Age was a key defeat, both for states' rights and for youth rights. A massive public relations battle was fought by MADD and opponents had no time to prepare before this battle was won. This legislation affects millions of people every day, as it has since it was passed in 1984.

> *"Common sense dictates that the legislatures of all other states and the Congress would never have passed such laws without a reasonable basis."*

The Minimum Drinking Age of Twenty-One Is Justified

The Louisiana Supreme Court's Decision

Jeffrey P. Victory

In 1995, Louisiana outlawed the sale of alcohol to eighteen- to twenty-year-olds to comply with the national minimum drinking age and avoid the loss of federal highway funds. Several individuals and retailers filed a suit against Louisiana in Manuel v. State, *and the trial court found the act discriminatory. The Louisiana Supreme Court affirmed that decision, but reversed its opinion on rehearing. In the following viewpoint, Justice Jeffrey P. Victory asserts that the drinking age of twenty-one is justified. He claims that it furthers the state's interest of highway safety, as evidence demonstrates that eighteen- to twenty-year-olds are involved in drunk-driving accidents at a disproportionate rate. Alternatives such as a total prohibition on alcohol or designating eighteen- to twenty-year-olds as minors are not feasible, he contends. Victory has served as an associate justice for the Louisiana Supreme Court since 1995.*

Jeffrey P. Victory, Opinion, *Manuel v. State*, Louisiana Supreme Court, March 8, 1996.

Article 1, Section 3, of the 1974 Louisiana Constitution allows laws to discriminate against persons because of their age, so long as the law does not "arbitrarily, capriciously, or unreasonably discriminate." *Sibley* [*v. LSU Board of Supervisors*] correctly interpreted this language to mean that the classification had to have a "reasonable basis." *Sibley* first explained that this burden is met by showing that the classification reasonably furthers a legitimate state purpose. However, within one paragraph, the test was expanded to "*substantially* furthers an *appropriate* state purpose." In early 1995, this Court in *Pace* [*v. State*] again expanded the requirement by holding that the classification must "substantially further an *important* governmental objective."

Examining Several Factors

The majority in the instant case, citing *Pace*, has again expanded the test, stating that Louisiana courts examine several factors, *including* whether: (1) each interest asserted by the state is actually implicated by the classifications employed in the statutory scheme; (2) there are no reasonable nondiscriminatory alternatives to the challenged statutory scheme by which the state's asserted interests and objectives might be satisfied; and (3) the discriminatory classifications contained in the challenged statutory scheme do not undercut any other countervailing state interest.

Further, the majority has now decided:

> We hold today, as explained *infra* [below] that in the context of a law which singles out a particular age group of adults for treatment different under the law from other adults, the classification can *only* be found constitutional if it is *the* classification which *most directly implicates* or furthers the asserted governmental interest. In other words, if the evidence shows there are other age groups which would better further the State's asserted interest, then the classification chosen is inherently arbitrary, capricious and unreasonable where there are no other asserted State interests which would justify choosing

the challenged classification over the group which better furthers the asserted State interest.

In my view, this Court in its prior cases, and the majority in this case, have distorted what Article 1, Section 3, actually means. As so eloquently stated by [delegate Chris] Roy at the Constitutional Convention, the phrase "no law shall arbitrarily, capriciously, or unreasonably discriminate against a person because of . . . age" simply means that the "state must show a reasonable basis for it." Thus, the state may meet its burden of proof by showing that the classification reasonably furthers any legitimate state purpose. Today [March 8, 1996] the majority raises the standard so that reasonableness can only be met if, in the subjective judgment of the majority, the legislature's choice to further highway safety is the best one, i.e., it most directly implicates or furthers the asserted governmental interest.

Youth Involvement in Auto-Related Accidents

The undisputed evidence produced by the state shows beyond question that the Legislature was not arbitrary, capricious, or unreasonable in passing this Act, because it reasonably furthers the state interest of highway safety. The majority acknowledges that the state's evidence shows that *nationwide*, drinking laws, such as at issue here, have been proven to save lives. FARS [Fatality Analysis Reporting System] data and studies show an over involvement of eighteen- to twenty-year-olds in alcohol-related car crashes, such as: (1) in 1994, 44% of traffic fatalities involving eighteen- to twenty-year-olds were alcohol-related, as compared to 40.8% for all traffic fatalities; (2) alcohol-related traffic fatality rates, on a per capita basis, are over twice as great for eighteen- to twenty-year-olds as for the population over twenty-one years old; (3) in 1994, more eighteen- to twenty-year-olds died in low-blood alcohol level (.01 to .09) traffic accidents than any other three-year age group; and (4) Louisiana had the fourth highest percentage of alcohol-related traffic fatalities of fifteen- to twenty-

Proponents of the higher minimum drinking age argue that it is needed because teens are more likely to be involved in drunk-driving accidents than older drivers. © Roy Morsch/ Corbis.

year-olds of all states. A 1989 National Highway Transportation Safety Administration study estimated that minimum drinking age laws have been responsible for a 12% reduction in fatal crash involvements of drivers affected by such laws, and NHTSA estimated in 1994 that minimum drinking age laws have reduced traffic fatalities involving eighteen- to twenty-year-olds by 13% and have saved an estimated 14,816 lives nationwide since 1975. The majority simply dismisses all of this undisputed factual information as irrelevant. Although sufficient for Congress to justify enacting the National Minimum Drinking [Age] Act, the majority erroneously discards the evidence and states that the only relevant inquiry in this case is the "greatest *number* of alcohol-related accidents *in Louisiana.*"

Yet the State presented compelling evidence about *Louisiana* accidents. 1986 Louisiana traffic records data reports compiled by the Louisiana Highway Safety Commission clearly show that eighteen- to twenty-year-old drivers had fatal and injury-producing accidents at the rate of 1 for every 191 drivers in that age group, whereas all other age groups had a *substantially higher* per capita rate of fatal and injury-producing accidents. The next closest group, the twenty-one– to twenty-four–year-olds, had a per capita rate of 1 out of every 217 drivers. This statistic showed that drivers in the eighteen- to twenty-year-old age group have fatal and injury-producing accidents at a 12% higher rate than the next highest group, the twenty-one– to twenty-four–year-old age group. Further, [former executive director of the Louisiana Highway Safety Commission Bette] Theis's affidavit that eighteen- to twenty-year-old drivers were only 5% of the licensed drivers in Louisiana in 1993 but were involved in 10% of the alcohol-related and fatal injury accidents, also clearly shows a much higher per capita rate for eighteen- to twenty-year-olds for alcohol-involved and fatal and injury car crashes. Again, the majority erroneously dismisses this evidence simply because the twenty-one– to twenty-four–year-old group has a higher *number* of drivers, thus resulting in a total *number* of fatal and injury accidents greater for that age group than the eighteen- to twenty-year-old group.

In spite of this overwhelming and compelling statistical evidence which clearly shows the Act does not arbitrarily, capriciously, or unreasonably discriminate based on age, the majority holds that the trial court was not manifestly erroneous in concluding as a factual matter that the state's interest in highway safety is not substantially furthered by the Act. The majority points to statistical evidence, such as eighteen- to twenty-year-olds are neither *arrested* in greater numbers in Evangeline Parish than other age groups for DWI [driving while intoxicated], and eighteen- to twenty-year-olds are not the age group with the highest incident of DWI *convictions* in Evangeline Parish. This evidence is easily explained by the fact that eighteen- to twenty-year-olds only make up 5% of the drivers. For instance, [paralegal Mary Jane] Marcantel's statistics for 1986 show 9 of 92 DWI arrests in Evangeline Parish were eighteen- to twenty-year-olds, *over 10% of the total arrests.* Her statistics for 1994-95 reveal 10 of 179 arrests for eighteen- to twenty-year-olds, which is 5.6% of the total arrests, larger than the percent of 5% for eighteen- to twenty-year-old drivers in Louisiana. Even if Marcantel's statistics had shown fewer arrests per capita for eighteen- to twenty-year-olds, there are many explanations as to why eighteen- to twenty-year-olds may not be arrested or convicted as frequently as other age groups including: (1) there are fewer eighteen- to twenty-year-old drivers; (2) police officers may be less inclined to arrest young adults for DWI, preferring to take them home instead; and (3) the fewer the arrests, the fewer the convictions. In my view, the evidence presented for arrests in Evangeline Parish *supports* the reasonableness of the Act because it shows more *per capita* arrests for eighteen- to twenty-year-olds than any other three-year age group.

Nondiscriminatory Alternatives

Having concluded that the trial court was not manifestly erroneous in finding that the state failed to carry its burden of proof that highway safety is not substantially furthered by the Act, the majority turns its attention to whether or not there are reasonable nondiscriminatory alternatives to the challenged statutory scheme by which the state's asserted interests and objectives might be satisfied. The majority suggests to avoid losing federal funding that the state could: (1) impose an absolute prohibition on the purchase, sale or possession of alcohol beverages of all persons of all ages in the state; or (2) raise the age of majority in the state to twenty-one so that eighteen- to twenty-year-olds would then be minors and would be subject to treatment as such. The majority's first suggestion, prohibition, conjures up the days of speak-easys, tommy-guns, and illegal importation of alcohol. Surely, it is an alternative that was tried and discarded decades ago. The majority's second suggestion that eighteen- to twenty-year-olds be reclassified by the Legislature to be minors, not

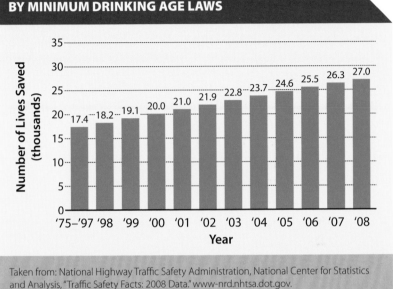

CUMULATIVE ESTIMATED NUMBER OF LIVES SAVED BY MINIMUM DRINKING AGE LAWS

Taken from: National Highway Traffic Safety Administration, National Center for Statistics and Analysis, "Traffic Safety Facts: 2008 Data." www-nrd.nhtsa.dot.gov.

adults, would not only deprive them of all of the other advantages that they gained by being classified as adults at age eighteen, but would also raise serious equal protection problems under the majority's own test herein. Would not a law to reclassify eighteen- to twenty-year-olds as minors simply to deny them the right to drink alcohol be arbitrary, capricious, and unreasonable under the majority's determination that state highway safety is not substantially furthered by denying them the right to drink?

In summary, every state (but Louisiana) and the federal government have drinking laws similar to the one in question. Common sense dictates that the legislatures of another states and the Congress would never have passed such laws without a reasonable basis. The reasons are obvious—traffic safety. The undisputed evidence introduced by the state shows that Louisiana drivers in the age group of eighteen- to twenty-year-olds have a much greater frequency of fatal and injury-producing accidents than any other three-year age group. The trial court was not free to disregard or minimize this evidence nor is this Court. In my view, the evidence presented shows a reasonable basis for the law, and the legislature did not arbitrarily, capriciously, and unreasonably discriminate against the eighteen- to twenty-year-olds. I would reverse the trial court's ruling of unconstitutionality and dismiss plaintiffs' claims.

"I learned my lesson the hard way when I could have taken it from others who already made that mistake."

A High School Student Learns a Difficult Lesson About Having a Party with Alcohol

Personal Narrative

Allie Rich

In the following viewpoint, a high school student relates the hard lessons she learned from hosting a "kegger" at her family's home. She did not drink, but she had to deal with the chaos and reckless- ness of other teens drinking in her home. Furthermore, her father returned before she could send everyone away. Making matters worse, one young man was too drunk to leave and had to stay the night. She reflects upon her mistake to have the alcohol-fueled party and asserts that the experience has deterred her from under- age drinking and making other poor choices. At the time of publi- cation, Allie Rich was a student in Knoxville, Tennessee.

High school parties—you have experienced them, heard stories, or watched movies about them. All in all, they are a plot for disaster. I am no superwoman, and I should have known that the story would be the same for me. I learned my lesson the hard way when I could have taken it from others who already made that mistake.

There I was, heart beating 50 miles an hour, left hand gripping a bottle of all-purpose cleaner, right hand holding a roll of paper towels, storming around my mobbed house cleaning up every mess I came across. Along the way I tried to hide anything fragile or of value. The smell of greasy potato chips and alcohol filled the air. The music was booming so loudly that I felt it in every part of my body.

"It'll be just a few friends, don't worry!" my friend had insisted earlier that day. This line replayed in my mind as I forced my way through the rowdy crowd that now filled my usually spacious living room. "Calm down, stop cleaning, and have a drink!" my friend called, attempting to put me at ease.

"You know I don't drink!" I growled. I was nervous, and everyone could tell. I had never been good at putting on a calm facade. It was 11 P.M., and my dad had left for his usual riverside hangout just three hours earlier. The party was in full swing and the house was a wreck. The kitchen table was covered in red plastic cups and paper plates, the cream-colored pool table was being used as a bench and beer stand, and the Mexican-tiled floors were covered in spilled drinks.

A Futile Cleanup Attempt

At that moment I looked like a "mommy" cleaning up and yelling at everyone to be careful not to spill, quiet down, and stop making a mess. "Please, *please* don't sit on that!" I yelled to the woozy skater boy propped on the bar. He replied with a laugh and continued flirting with a girl in a pink miniskirt.

I was drained, and I wish I had opted to get in my comfy PJs, pop some kettle corn, and watch "Love Actually" for the millionth time. I closed my eyes, took a deep breath, and accepted my fate. I stepped out the back door to the pool area.

"One . . . two . . . THREE!" Two oversized, immature boys pitched their victim in the pool. "What do you think you're doing?" I yelled. Once again, I received only a laugh in reply. I was starting to wonder if I might be invisible, but that thought quickly passed when the boys grabbed me and started the countdown again. Before I realized what was happening, I felt the cold rush of water around me. I was their latest victim.

I was soggy and now officially miserable. That was the last straw. I had to think of a plan to get everyone out of the house. I went inside and found one of my brother's larger friends, Jake, and asked him for help.

"I need you and whatever decent friends you have to get *everyone* out of this house," I commanded, and then I threw in some inspiration. "I don't know if you remember, but my dad resembles Rambo . . . and he's on his way home!" He really does look like Rambo, and I actually had no idea when he would be back, so it could have been true.

Not Soon Enough

This definitely sunk in, and before I knew it, Jake was yelling, "Everyone out!" This triggered a stampede. Kids were finally leaving, but not soon enough. Outside, I heard an engine. My dad was pulling up in his boat with four friends. My heart began to race, and I ran to defend myself. When I reached my dad, I saw his expression change as he realized what was going on.

"Allie, how did this happen?" he asked. I sank inside my invisible turtle shell to think of an explanation. "Tell me later, after we fix this," he added, cutting me off. My dad walked to the pool area where the kids who hadn't gotten the message were still partying. "Everyone get off my property and go *home!*" he bellowed. Those who were sober enough to understand fell silent, and in a matter of five minutes they had all left by way of cars, skateboards, bicycles, or their running feet.

But it wasn't over yet. Lying in the yard was a boy who was obviously drunk—so much so that he was incomprehensible. He had on a bathing suit and one shoe. My dad and his friend picked him up, took him inside, and deposited him on the couch. We spent hours trying to elicit understandable information. He kept repeating the same number over and over, but it didn't work. It became clear that he would have to stay the night.

While this was going on, I rushed my friend to my room and told her to brush her teeth, wash her face, and hit the sack. She was drunk and desperately needed to sleep it off. It had been a long night, and it was hard for me even to look at my dad. He told me to go to bed; we would talk in the morning. I fell right to sleep and dreamed that all was well and I had just watched "Love Actually" with a bowl of kettle corn.

Facing the Aftermath

When I awoke the next morning, reality sank in again. I was miserable, tired, and knew the fate to come. I stumbled out of bed and went straight to the bathroom. I decided to look fresh and presentable for this discussion with my dad.

As I walked into the living room, I saw my dad sitting next to the mystery boy who was now sober. My dad looked up and said, "I am very disappointed in you. I always say that you should learn from my mistakes. I have told you my stories many times, and you know how they end."

With my dad, nothing is worse than disappointing him. At this moment, I realized that it is smarter to learn from the mistakes of others than to make them yourself. My dad took home the one-shoed boy and talked with his parents. He also called my friend's parents, who picked her up with disappointment on their faces. We all learned our lesson.

This happened a year and a half ago, and since then I have thought things through, understand the idea of consequences, and now learn from the mistakes of others. Why smoke when I know I'll get addicted? Why drink at my age when I know that I could end up doing something stupid? As [H.G. Wells] said, "Wise men learn by other men's mistakes, fools by their own."

"If we are serious about embracing [the founders'] vision of a free society . . . repeal the national minimum drinking age law."

The Minimum Drinking Age Should Be Lowered

Jeffrey A. Tucker

In the following viewpoint, Jeffrey A. Tucker urges the US Congress to repeal the minimum drinking age of twenty-one. Tucker asserts that the law is ineffective in the deterrence of underage drinking and creates an industry of fake IDs. Contrary to widely accepted statistics, Tucker argues, the law has neither lowered the rates of drunken driving nor drinking among college students. As a result, he views the minimum drinking age as an arbitrary imposition on liberty that teaches young people to flout the law. Tucker is editorial vice president of Mises.org, the website of the Ludwig von Mises Institute, a libertarian think tank.

Somehow, and no one seems to even imagine how, this country managed to survive and thrive before 1984 without a national minimum drinking age. Before that, the drinking question was left to the states.

In the 19th century, and looking back even before—prepare yourself to imagine horrific anarchistic nightmares—there were no drinking laws anywhere, so far as anyone can tell. The regulation of drinking and age was left to society, which is to say families, churches, and communities with varying sensibilities who regulated such things with varying degrees of intensity. Probably some kids drank themselves silly, and we all know that this doesn't happen now (wink, wink), but many others learned to drink responsibly from an early age, even drinking bourbon for breakfast.

Finding Ways Around Restrictions

Really, it is only because we are somehow used to it that we accept the complete absurdity of a national law that prohibits the sale of beer, wine, and liquor to anyone under the age of 21. Every day, the police are busting up parties, shutting down bars, hectoring restaurants, fining convenience stores, and otherwise bullying people into clean living. We read the news and think: crazy kids; they shouldn't be doing this.

And yet every day, young people are finding ways around these preposterous restrictions that are hardly ever questioned, imbibing with their booze a disdain for the law and a creative spirit of criminality, along with a disposition to binge drink when their legal workarounds succeed.

On college campuses, the industry of the fake ID thrives as never before. It seems nearly true that almost every student believes himself or herself in need of getting one. Do the restaurants and bars know this? Of course they do. They have every interest in having these fake IDs look as real as possible to give themselves some degree of legal immunity if someone gets caught. The whole thing is a gigantic fakeroo, a mass exercise in open but unspoken hypocrisy, and everyone knows it.

If you think about it, it is the very definition of a state gone mad that a society would have a law of this sort spread out over an entire nation that tells people that they cannot drink before

the age of 21 even as most everyone in a position to do so happily breaks the law. In Virginia in the Colonial period, where the average lifespan was 25, this law would have provided only 4 years of drinking in the last fifth of one's life (but what a way to go).

However, if you think about the history of this country in the twentieth century, one might say that the age of 21 is actually rather liberal, as strange as that may sound. After all, it was in this country, the "land of the free," that the federal government actually added as part of its Constitution a total banning of liquor, wine, and beer from sea to shining sea (1920 to 1933). The 1920s roared in any case, with organized crime, speakeasies, police corruption, rampant criminality and alcohol abuse.

The Mystery of Prohibition

The mystery to me is not the failure of Prohibition but the sheer insanity of the attempt to do this in the first place. It seems utterly bizarre in a country that habitually proclaims its devotion to liberty and freedom that such a thing would have ever been attempted. But here is Amendment XVIII, passed in 1917, in the same epoch in which government was going to rid the world of despotism and stabilize all business cycle through scientific monetary policy: "the manufacture, sale, or transportation of intoxicating liquors within, the importation thereof into, or the exportation thereof from the United States and all territory subject to the jurisdiction thereof for beverage purposes is hereby prohibited."

Yes, it really happened, right here in the good ol' USA, and I'm grateful to [economist] Mark Thornton for documenting the politics and economics of the whole sad affair in his book *The Economics of Prohibition*. In a rare case of reversion and admission of error, the same constitution was later amended again: "The eighteenth article of amendment to the Constitution of the United States is hereby repealed."

But the habit of Prohibition was already ingrained. For the state, it was two steps forward and one step back. For the rest of the population, what was previously a very normal part of life, drinking potentially intoxicating liquids, something integral to normal living from the Paleolithic era forward, took on a special ethos of hipness and derring-do. The father of our country might have been the largest distiller of whiskey in the late 1700s, but after Prohibition, liquor took on associations with decadence and bad behavior generally. A distiller today wouldn't be elected to the City Council much less as the U.S. President.

Now, it wasn't too many years ago that the laws tended to be a bit more reasonable, with the drinking age starting at 18. But that was changed with a universal law for the age of 21, and many people remember what this was like: for two years, a person was able to order a beer with a burger and, then one day, doing the same thing was a criminal act.

The Overarching Argument of Drinking and Driving

Digging around for explanations about these silly laws, there is one overarching argument: driving. We don't want drunk teenagers on the road. These laws have saved thousands, millions, of lives, and the desire to change them is the equivalent of harboring a death wish for a generation. Now, one libertarian response might be: then get rid of the public roads and let road owners manage whether and to what extent its drivers drink. That's a principled position but a bit impractical. The biggest problem with that response is that it concedes too much.

The closer you look at these studies, the more fishy they appear. It turns [out] that most of the declines in binge drinking among High School kids, according to a trends in drug use report, took place before the change in the law, and, according to researchers Jeffrey A. Miron and Elina Tetelbaum, the changes in trends after are heavily biased by data sampling from a single state. Therefore, data on drunk driving, whatever the trends, cannot be statistically attributed to the national minimum drinking age law.

In any case, drinking is still sky high, even with the law, making cause and effect even more difficult to trace. As to why drinking is still high among college students, The National Institute on Drug Abuse offers the following polite reason: "campuses provided some insulation from the effects of changes in the drinking age laws that took place during that interval." You can say that again. Human beings are remarkable things: when they want to do something, no amount of tyranny, even that of jail, can stop them.

Still, it is impossible to silence the screams of the prohibition advocates, who trace every car accident among teen drivers to alcohol. I find this all fascinating to read because it bears so much in common with the Prohibition literature from the 1910s and 1920s. Their propaganda blamed alcohol for the destruction of the family, the persistence of poverty, the high rate of crime, the problem of illiteracy, and the ubiquity of sin generally. Clearly, their arguments were widely accepted even though it is all a big and fallacious mix up of cause and effect. It's not that liquor caused all these terrible things; it's that the people who engage in

College students in Arizona fill cups from a keg at a party. Critics of the national minimum drinking age say that it is ineffective at curbing teen drinking. © Mark Peterson/Corbis.

terrible behaviors tend to also be drinkers. Abolishing the drink won't fix the problems of the human heart.

So it is with teenage drinking. With the two-thirds and more of people under the age of 21 reporting that they have consumed alcohol in the last year, it should be obvious that the law is doing nothing but providing a gigantic excuse for arbitrary police-state impositions on human liberty, and also socializing young people in a habit of hypocrisy and law breaking. It's like the old Soviet-style joke: they pretend to regulate us and we pretend to be regulated.

Still, shouldn't it be illegal for young people to drink and drive? [Economist] Murray Rothbard sums up the libertarian point in *For a New Liberty*: "Only the overt commission of a crime should be illegal, and the way to combat crimes committed under the influence of alcohol is to be more diligent about the crimes themselves, not to outlaw the alcohol. And this would have the further beneficial effect of reducing crimes *not* committed under the influence of alcohol."

Repeal the Minimum Drinking Age

We've just been through our annual celebration of Independence Day, the day on which every radio and television commentator gives pious speeches about the glories of American liberty and all the sacrifices that have been made to preserve it.

Do we really believe it? The founders would have never imagined such a thing as a national law regulating the age at which beer, wine, port, and other alcoholic beverages are consumed. If we are serious about embracing their vision of a free society, as opposed to just blathering about it, let's start with something that is supremely practical and would have immediate effects on an entire generation: repeal the national minimum drinking age law.

You say that this is unthinkable? I say that you don't really believe in human liberty.

"Policymakers might more effectively address not whether a change in the legal age is warranted but, rather, what measures will make current policy more effective."

The Minimum Drinking Age Should Not Be Lowered

Noah Ives

In the following viewpoint, Noah Ives contends that the minimum drinking age should not be lowered. He opposes arguments that a drinking age of eighteen would end the underground consumption of alcohol, deter youths from driving to covert venues to drink, and reduce binge drinking. Instead, Ives says the evidence suggests that lowering the drinking age would not impact overall consumption, risky youth drinking, or other harms related to alcohol. In fact, he points out, the rates in Europe—where drinking laws are generally more permissive—reveal that youth there actually drink more often and more heavily. At the time of publication, Ives was a graduate student assistant at the University of Wisconsin Population Health Institute.

Legislatures in seven states have recently introduced bills that would lower the legal drinking age from 21 to 18. In addition, a group of college and university presidents recently called

Empty alcohol bottles fill trash bins in central London. In Europe, where drinking laws are more permissive, the rate of alcohol abuse by young people is higher than in the United States. © AP Images/Alastair Grant.

for a reconsideration of the 21 year old drinking age. The probable effects of such a change have sparked considerable debate. Supporters argue that a lower drinking age would encourage responsible consumption. Critics anticipate higher rates of consumption, risky drinking and drinking and driving.

Besides the potential effect on drinking among young people, the debate involves other practical and ideological issues. Proponents of a lower age question the legality of denying the right to drink to legal adults—especially to those who serve in the military. Yet it would be difficult for states to lower their drinking ages below 21, as they would lose 10% of their federal highway funds. Nonetheless, prominent public dialogue has renewed the need to consider whether current policy serves our public health goals and citizenship rights.

Why Is the Legal Drinking Age Twenty-One?

Individual states have set their own minimum drinking ages since the end of Prohibition in 1933. Most states initially chose 21, though several set it at 18. During the Vietnam War, however, nearly every state embraced the principle that a person old enough to serve in the military should have the full rights of citizenship. Most states lowered the age of legal adulthood from 21 to 18, and 30 states lowered the legal drinking age along with it.

Following this change, a number of studies demonstrated high rates of risky drinking and related harms among young people. Lobbying groups, most notably Mothers Against Drunk Driving (MADD), formed to petition for a higher minimum age. The National Minimum Drinking Age Act of 1984 passed, requiring all states to raise the drinking age to 21 or lose 10% of their federal highway funds. By 1987, all 50 states had adopted a minimum age of 21. In Wisconsin, an underage person is prohibited from consuming an alcoholic beverage unless accompanied by a parent, guardian or spouse who has attained the legal drinking age.

Current Impetus for Change

Long-standing evidence suggests that alcohol consumption and related harms declined sharply following the National Minimum Drinking Age Act. But, recently the strength of the evidence has been called into question. High rates of drinking-related harm persist among young people, and this has led to questions about whether the current policy comes with unintended negative consequences.

The current movement for change is fueled by ideological questions. Choose Responsibility, a non-profit organization founded in 2007, points out that the drinking age is the only exception to the legal age of adulthood, and argues that 18-year-olds, as U.S. citizens, should be given full rights. These advocates call for regulation by parents and guardians rather than the government. Particular concerns persist about limiting the rights of members of the armed forces. This concept is not new: military bases abroad or within 50 miles of Mexico or Canada may adopt drinking ages lower than 21.

Recent proposals in South Dakota, Missouri, Vermont and Minnesota would reduce the drinking to age 18 for all state residents, while in Kentucky, Wisconsin and South Carolina they would reduce the age only for members of the military. Other discussion now focuses on harm reduction strategies and on other countries' policies that do not rely on alcohol abstinence for young people.

Evidence for Current Policy

Extensive research shows, and leading health organizations agree, that both drinking and drinking-related harm among young people declined significantly following the National Minimum Drinking Age Act. A New York survey found as much as a 25% decrease in alcohol consumption among 18, 19 and 20 year olds. The National Highway and Traffic Institute estimates that, after raising the minimum drinking age, drivers under age 21 experienced 12% fewer fatal crashes. Studies conducted in European countries have reinforced these U.S. findings.

Some recent analyses, however, suggest that minimum age laws may have had substantially less impact than previously believed. The statistical decline in drinking-related fatalities represents the cumulative effect of many changes. These include safety improvements such as seat belt laws and safer vehicle design, along with increased law enforcement and public education. The higher drinking age did separate the experiential learning period (including higher collision and fatality rates) for newly licensed drivers from that of newly legal drinkers, though the importance of separating these two acculturation periods is not clear. Later drinking age, and later acculturation to legal drinking, may simply shift the attendant mortality risks to later young adulthood.

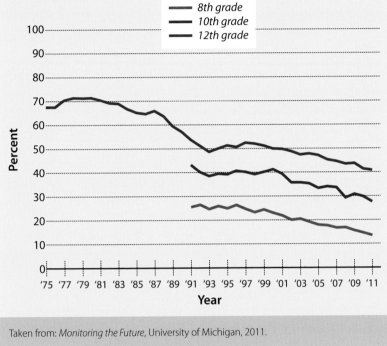

A STEADY DECLINE IN ALCOHOL USE BY TEENS

This graph shows the percentage of students who used alcohol in the last thirty days.

Taken from: *Monitoring the Future*, University of Michigan, 2011.

Evidence for a Lower Drinking Age

High rates of drinking-related harm persist among young people, and this has led to questions about whether the current policy comes with unintended negative consequences. Traffic fatalities are the leading cause of teen deaths, over 20% of which, involved alcohol over the past decade. Current U.S. policy, critics argue, drives alcohol consumption underground with no regulation; underage drinkers drink in private rather than in bars, with no parental or other adult supervision. Some suggest that teens' quest for covert drinking venues may compel them to drive, and encourages teens to consume more per drinking occasion than do adults. Over 90% of alcohol consumed by underage drinkers is consumed in an episode of binge drinking, a danger particularly apparent among college students.

Still, very little evidence suggests that [a] lower minimum drinking age would reduce overall consumption, risky drinking among youths, or drinking related harms. The oft-cited lower rate of alcohol-related traffic fatalities among young people in Europe—countries with more permissive laws—is likely due to lower rates of driving among European youth in general. Similarly, although there are lower binge drinking rates among youth in some European countries, European youth overall both drink more and drink more heavily than in the US.

Making the Current Policy More Effective

Advocacy groups have rallied on both sides of this issue. Last year [in 2007], MADD, along with the American Medical Association, the National Transportation Safety Board and the Insurance Institute for Highway Safety formed Support 21 to maintain the current drinking age. On the other side of the debate, the National Youth Rights Association and Choose Responsibility argue for lowering the minimum age.

A 2007 Gallup Poll found that 77% of Americans oppose lowering the drinking age to 18. Some suggest that the choice be left to states. But the uniform federal standard, as defined by the National Minimum Drinking Age Act, prevails over individual state choice in order to prevent the likelihood that underage drinkers would purchase alcohol in neighboring states, and compound the risk of harm by driving to do so.

It will always be a challenge to enforce a minimum age in a culture where alcohol is so widely marketed and consumed. There may be an unavoidable trade-off between telling young people that they cannot drink and keeping them safe when they do so anyway. Yet the Institute of Medicine has concluded that "the effectiveness of laws to restrict access to alcohol by youths can be increased by closing gaps in coverage, promoting compliance, and strengthening enforcement." Given the current evidence, policymakers might more effectively address not whether a change in the legal age is warranted but, rather, what measures will make current policy more effective.

> "If this court were to adopt social host liability, we would be faced with determining under which of the many possible permutations liability would lie."

Social Hosts Are Not Liable for Serving Alcohol

The Illinois Supreme Court's Decision

Thomas R. Fitzgerald

In 1997, sixteen-year-old Elizabeth Wakulich died after brothers Michael and Brian Mraz dared her to drink a bottle of liquor, did not seek medical attention, and prevented others from doing so when she fell unconscious. In Wakulich v. Mraz, *her mother alleged negligence in serving alcohol to a minor and the voluntary undertaking of her care. The Illinois Supreme Court reviewed the case on appeal. In the following viewpoint, Justice Thomas R. Fitzgerald claims that Illinois law states that social hosts serving alcohol, whether to adults or minors, are not liable. If the court recognized such a liability, Fitzgerald states, it would be too broadly applied and flood the legal system. Nonetheless, he argues that the Mrazs are liable of negligence in Wakulich's care, as they took complete and exclusive charge of her duty and actively prevented others*

Thomas R. Fitzgerald, Opinion, *Wakulich v. Mraz*, Illinois Supreme Court, February 6, 2003.

from seeking medical help. Fitzgerald is former chief justice of the Illinois Supreme Court.

Following the death of her 16-year-old daughter Elizabeth Wakulich, plaintiff Mary Louise Wakulich, individually and as special administrator of Elizabeth's estate, brought an action in the circuit court of Cook County, alleging claims under the Wrongful Death Act and the Survival Act. According to the 10-count "Amended Second Amended Complaint," during the evening of June 15, 1997, and continuing into the early morning hours of June 16, 1997, Elizabeth was at the home of defendants, Michael Mraz, his brother Brian Mraz, and their father Dennis Mraz. At that time, Michael was 21 years old, and Brian was 18 years old. Plaintiff alleged that Michael and Brian induced Elizabeth, "by offering monies, by goading and by applying great social pressure," to drink a quart bottle of Goldschlager, a "highly alcoholic and dangerous" beverage, and that Michael and Brian knew, or should have known, that Elizabeth, a minor, could not appreciate the dangers associated with consumption of excessive amounts of alcoholic beverages.

According to the complaint, after consuming the entire bottle of Goldschlager, Elizabeth lost consciousness. Michael and Brian placed her in the family room of their home, where they observed her "vomiting profusely and making gurgling sounds." They later removed her vomit-saturated blouse and placed a pillow under her head to prevent aspiration. Brian and Michael allegedly refused to drive Elizabeth home, did not contact her parents, did not seek medical attention, and "actually prevented other individuals at the home from calling 911 or seeking other medical intervention." Plaintiff further alleged in the complaint that, during the morning of June 16, 1997, Dennis "ordered" Michael and Brian to remove Elizabeth from their home, which they did. Elizabeth died later that day. The complaint indicates that Michael was subsequently convicted of contributing to the delinquency of a minor.

Plaintiff advanced two theories of recovery: (1) that Michael and Brian were negligent in providing alcohol to Elizabeth and inducing her to drink to excess (counts I, II, V and VI); and (2) that Michael, Brian and Dennis were negligent in failing to act reasonably to protect Elizabeth after voluntarily undertaking to care for her after she lost consciousness (counts III, IV, VII, VIII, IX and X). . . .

The Illinois Supreme Court Does Not Recognize Social Host Liability

We consider first those counts which alleged that Michael and Brian were negligent in providing an alcoholic beverage to Elizabeth and inducing her to consume a dangerous amount. Defendants contend that these counts were properly dismissed based on our decision in *Charles v. Seigfried.*

In *Charles*, decided just two years prior to the events giving rise to the present litigation, we addressed whether this court should recognize a cause of action against social hosts for serving alcoholic beverages to minors who are subsequently injured. The factual backdrop against which we decided this issue involved two different social gatherings at which minors were served alcoholic beverages, became intoxicated, and were involved in motor vehicle accidents. In the first case, Lynn Sue Charles, who was 16 years of age at the time, became intoxicated at the defendant's home. She left the party by driving her own automobile and was later involved in a fatal collision. In the second case [*Bzdek v. Townsley*], 15-year-old Paula Bzdek became intoxicated at the defendants' home, and left the party with an 18-year-old friend, who was also intoxicated. The 18-year-old friend lost control of his vehicle, crashing into oncoming traffic. Bzdek, who was a passenger in the vehicle, suffered permanent injuries. In each case, a complaint was filed premised on theories of social host liability. In each case, the trial court dismissed the complaint, the plaintiff appealed, and the appellate court reversed the dismissal.

In the *Charles* litigation, the appellate court recognized a cause of action against a social host who knowingly serves alcoholic beverages to a minor at the social host's residence, permits the minor to become intoxicated, and allows the minor to leave in a motor vehicle. "In the *Bzdek* litigation, the appellate court recognized a similar cause of action against social hosts who knowingly serve intoxicants to persons under the legal drinking age of 21. In a consolidated appeal, we reversed both decisions. Relying on over a century of precedent, we held that "Illinois has no common law cause of action for injuries arising out of the sale or gift of alcoholic beverages; that the legislature has preempted the field of alcohol-related liability; and that any change in the law governing alcohol-related liability should be made by the General Assembly, or not at all." We thus declined to adopt any form of social host liability.

The Dramshop Act and Liability

In the instant case, plaintiff requests that we reconsider and overrule *Charles* and recognize a common law negligence action against adult social hosts, *i.e.*, persons 18 years of age and older who knowingly serve alcohol to a minor. Based on the doctrine of *stare decisis* [standing by precedents established in previous court decisions], we deny plaintiff's request and adhere to our decision in *Charles*. . . .

Plaintiff argues, for example, that this court should follow the "national trend" recognizing a cause of action against adult social hosts who provide alcohol to minors. We expressly rejected this argument in *Charles*, concluding that our decision should be "grounded upon the law of Illinois rather than upon contradictory trends elsewhere." As explained in *Charles*, in Illinois, the common law recognized no cause of action for injuries arising out of the sale or gift of alcoholic beverages. The legislature's adoption of the Dramshop Act (now codified as section 6-21 of the Liquor Control Act of 1934) created a limited and exclusive statutory cause of action by imposing a form of no-fault liability upon dramshops [establishments that sell alcoholic beverages] for selling or giving intoxicating liquors to persons who subsequently injure third parties. Through its passage and continual amendment of the Dramshop Act, the General Assembly has preempted the entire field of alcohol-related liability.

Plaintiff in the instant case also argues that because Illinois law clearly treats minors as a "protected class" when it comes to the consumption of alcohol, tort liability should apply to adult social hosts who serve alcoholic beverages to minors. We considered and dismissed this very argument in *Charles*. "Legislative preemption in the field of alcohol-related liability extends to social hosts who provide alcoholic beverages to another person, *whether that person be an adult, an underage person, or a minor.*"

Judicial Restraint Is Appropriate

Plaintiff here further contends that "public policy" dictates that this court should recognize social host liability for the provision of alcohol to minors. In *Charles*, however, we observed that the "primary expression of Illinois public and social policy should emanate from the legislature." . . .

We held, therefore, that judicial restraint in this area was appropriate and that any decision to expand civil liability of social hosts should be made by the legislature.

Additionally, plaintiff argues that where, as here, the legislature has failed to act, it is the duty of this court to intervene and develop the common law. Once again, this is an argument that we expressly considered and rejected in *Charles*. We observed that, since 1986, the General Assembly had considered imposing some form of social host liability upon adults who furnish alcohol to underage persons at least six times, but that such attempts were rejected. We appropriately inferred that the General Assembly had deliberately chosen *not* to impose such social host liability.

Since our decision in *Charles*, the General Assembly has again considered imposing liability upon persons who supply

Young people drink in a private home. Some courts in the United States have ruled that hosts are not liable for accidents that may be caused by minors who drink and drive. © Alyson Aliano/Getty Images.

alcoholic beverages to minors. These attempts to create a new cause of action did not succeed. We do not view such failed attempts as inaction on the part of the legislature. Rather, we view it as evidence that the legislature continues to debate and consider the merits and contours of any form of social host liability. . . .

Opening the Flood Gates

Plaintiff maintains that she is not asking this court to "open the flood gates" regarding social-host liability. We note, however, that the cause of action plaintiff would have us recognize is broader than the proposed cause of action we declined to recognize in *Charles*. Under the facts of *Charles*, liability could have been limited to situations involving underage drunk driving. In the present case, however, plaintiff seeks to impose liability for *any* injuries proximately caused by the adult provision of alcoholic beverages to a minor. In addition, there was no indication in *Charles* that the social-host defendants were not themselves of legal drinking age. Plaintiff in the instant case, however, seeks to impose liability upon *any* adult social host, irrespective of whether the social host is of legal drinking age. Brian, the younger of the two remaining defendants, was only 18 years of age at the time of the underlying events, three years younger than the legal drinking age of 21 years. Thus, plaintiff actually proposes a broad and sweeping change to this area of the law by proposing that all adults—even those adults whom the General Assembly has determined are unable to appreciate sufficiently the risks attendant to alcohol consumption—may be liable in tort for any and all injuries flowing from the provision of alcohol to minors.

Even if the cause of action plaintiff would have us recognize in the present case was more narrowly tailored, we do not agree with plaintiff that the "flood gates" would not be opened. We recognized in *Charles* that the adoption of social host liability in that case would open up a "'Pandora's Box' of unlimited liability," as any person who might conceivably qualify as a social host was made the target of a lawsuit. We recognized also that, if this court were to adopt social host liability, we would be faced with determining under which of the many possible permutations liability would lie.

> Should only injured third parties have a cause of action against a social host, or should the intoxicated person have one too? Should an exception be created only for minors? If so, should we treat persons under the legal drinking age of 21 as minors, or only those under the age of 18? Should minor or underage social hosts be liable for serving liquor to their similarly situated friends? Should a social host be held liable only when he or she knows that the intoxicated person will drink and drive, or should the host be liable for all types of alcohol-induced injuries? What actions must a social host take to avoid liability where an intoxicated guest insists on driving home? Is calling a cab sufficient, or must the police be notified? *The flood of*

*injured litigants that would inevitably crowd the Illinois courts
would demand answers to these questions and many others.*

The adoption of social host liability in this case would likewise raise numerous questions to which the flood of litigants would demand answers. Should social hosts be liable only for "knowingly" providing alcohol to minors, or should the social host's conduct be judged by what he or she "should have known"? For example, should parents be liable for the consumption of alcoholic beverages in their home if they "should have known" that their 17-year-old child would have a party in their absence? What measures should parents take to ensure that access to liquor in the home is sufficiently restricted in order to avoid liability for illegal activities that occur in their absence? Should liability attach outside the home to social gatherings such as picnics, weddings and other events? Should the social host be liable even where the intoxicated minor's parents are present at the social gathering? Should liability attach where the minor consumes a negligible amount of alcohol, is clearly not intoxicated, but has an adverse reaction due to a medical condition unknown to the social host? Should the liability of social hosts be unlimited, or subject to the same limitation applicable to liquor vendors?

The members of our General Assembly, elected by the citizens of this state, are best able to resolve such issues comprehensively, taking into account the significant social and economic consequences of any course of action. They are best equipped to determine whether a change in the law is both desirable and workable, and if so, under what circumstances. Thus far, the General Assembly has determined that civil liability for alcohol-related injuries is limited to two groups of defendants: (1) dramshop owners, and (2) persons 21 years of age or older who pay for a hotel or motel room knowing that the room will be used by underage persons for the unlawful consumption of alcohol. The liability of these defendants is limited and extends only to third parties, and not to the intoxicated person. . . .

In sum, plaintiff has not provided any principled basis for this court to revisit its decision in *Charles* and depart from the doctrine of *stare decisis*. Plaintiff cannot identify any compelling change in circumstance since our decision was filed and has simply reargued points already considered and rejected. Accordingly, we adhere to our decision in *Charles*: apart from the limited civil liability provided in the Dramshop Act, there exists no social host liability in Illinois. . . .

The Voluntary Undertaking Theory of Liability

We next consider whether, as defendants argue, those counts of the complaint alleging a "voluntary undertaking" by Michael and Brian are fatally defective. Generally, pursuant to the voluntary undertaking theory of liability, "one who undertakes, gratuitously or for consideration, to render services to another is subject to liability for bodily harm caused to the other by one's failure to exercise due care in the performance of the undertaking." . . .

As an initial matter, defendants argue that plaintiff's voluntary undertaking theory is simply an attempt to circumvent the rule against social host liability set forth in *Charles*. This argument fails. The liability of defendants, if any, is not contingent on their status as social hosts. Indeed, it is irrelevant for purposes of plaintiff's voluntary undertaking counts whether defendants were acting as social hosts on the evening of June 15, 1997, and supplied the alcohol which Elizabeth consumed. Rather, based on the allegations of the complaint, defendants' liability arises by virtue of their voluntary assumption of a duty to care for Elizabeth after she became unconscious, irrespective of the circumstances leading up to that point. Thus, plaintiff's voluntary undertaking theory does not circumvent the rule against social host liability.

In a related argument, defendants maintain that there is no special relationship between a social host and a guest which would impose a duty upon the social host to seek medical assistance. This argument, like the one before it, necessarily fails.

Plaintiff did not allege that defendants were under a legal duty to seek medical assistance for Elizabeth, or to otherwise care for her, by virtue of their status as social hosts or their relationship with Elizabeth. Plaintiff alleged that defendants *voluntarily* undertook to care for Elizabeth. "By undertaking to act defendant[s] became subject to a duty with respect to the manner of performance." *Nelson v. Union Wire Rope Corp.* In other words, having undertaken to care for Elizabeth, defendants were obligated to exercise "due care" in the performance of that undertaking.

Defendants next argue that, even if this court accepts a voluntary undertaking theory of liability, their duty is limited to the extent of the undertaking. Defendants explain that where, as here, a host merely permits an intoxicated guest to "sleep it off" on the host's floor, the host does not thereby assume an open-ended duty to care for the guest and assess the guest's medical condition. Although we agree with these statements as a general proposition, based on the allegations of the complaint, defendants here did more than simply make their floor available to Elizabeth to "sleep it off." Rather, defendants placed her in the family room; checked on her periodically; took measures to prevent aspiration; removed her soiled blouse; and prevented other persons present in the home from intervening in Elizabeth's behalf. As alleged by plaintiffs, defendants effectively took complete and exclusive charge of Elizabeth's care after she became unconscious. . . .

Here, plaintiff has alleged that defendants failed to summon aid by contacting Elizabeth's parents, failed to otherwise obtain medical assistance that evening or the following morning when she was still unconscious, and prevented other persons from obtaining aid, proximately causing her death. These allegations, liberally construed, sufficiently allege that defendants' conduct "increased the risk of harm" to Elizabeth.

Not Simply a Failure to Act
Finally, defendants argue that their alleged failure to summon medical or other assistance constitutes mere "nonfeasance" and

that a breach of the duty imposed by reason of a voluntary undertaking can only be found where there is "misfeasance," unless the plaintiff can demonstrate reliance by the injured party. We agree that the case law frequently distinguishes between nonfeasance and misfeasance where a voluntary undertaking is alleged. Such distinction, however, does not insulate defendants from liability in this case. . . .

Importantly, plaintiff's theory in this case is *not* that defendants failed to perform *at all* and are liable for their nonfeasance. Plaintiff's theory is that defendants *negligently performed* their voluntary undertaking and are liable for their misfeasance. Although defendants' alleged failure to summon medical assistance is itself inaction, it is also one of the ways in which plaintiff claims defendants negligently performed their voluntary undertaking to care for Elizabeth, which is affirmative misconduct. . . .

In any event, defendants overlook that part of the complaint which states that defendants "actually prevented other individuals at the home from calling 911 or seeking other medical intervention." Thus, plaintiff has alleged an affirmative act by defendants, not simply a failure to act.

We conclude, as did the appellate court, that the allegations of plaintiff's complaint sufficiently stated a cause of action based on a voluntary undertaking theory and that counts III, IV, VII and VIII should not have been dismissed.

> *"While parents think that they are providing their kids with an exemplary and safe alternative to drunk driving, they are setting [a] dangerous example."*

Parents Should Be Liable When Minors Drink in Their Homes

William J. Bernat

In the following viewpoint, William J. Bernat maintains that parents who host parties with alcohol for their children should be liable, especially for the risks or harms to third parties as a result of drunken driving. Fatal car accidents involving teenagers and alcohol are on the rise, he contends, and legal sanctions do not dissuade parents from hosting such parties. Because teenagers lack the experience or maturity to know when to stop drinking, it leaves the parents or adults who serve alcohol to them solely responsible to prevent injuries to third parties, Bernat insists. Bernat is an associate at the law firm Nutter McClennen and Fish in Massachusetts.

William J. Bernat, "Party On?: The Excellent Adventures of Social Host Liability in Massachusetts," *Suffolk University Law Review*, vol. 39, 2006, pp. 981–986, 990–992, 994–996, 999. Copyright © 2006 by Suffolk University Law Review. All rights reserved. Reproduced by permission.

When Ronald and Carolyn Moulton let their daughter and several of her friends drink at their Danvers, Massachusetts home after their high school prom, they did not think that they were doing anything wrong. After all, they took away all of the teenagers' keys before allowing them to imbibe any of the numerous cases of beer and hard liquor. Ronald even joined them. Even after they were sentenced to forty hours of court-ordered community service, eighteen months of probation, and paid a five hundred dollar fine, the Moultons still contend that they did the right thing that night because no one got hurt. Unfortunately, they are not alone in that opinion.

With teenage fatalities skyrocketing in recent years due to alcohol related automobile accidents, the newest trend in teenage drinking is for parents to allow underage children to consume alcohol at home under their supervision. While parents think that they are providing their kids with an exemplary and safe alternative to drunk driving, they are setting the dangerous example that it is all right to pick and choose which laws to follow. Even more disturbing is that they do so with little more than a slap on the wrist, as current criminal and civil sanctions often do little to deter parents from hosting such parties.

Some states have begun clamping down on these underage parties by punishing the individuals responsible for allowing them to occur. Massachusetts, for example, has implemented harsher jail time and fines for parents who violate the criminal statute by allowing underage drinking in their homes. Massachusetts will not, however, extend civil liability to reach parents who do not actually furnish the alcohol if someone is subsequently injured by one of their guests. The result is a confusing and confounding social host area of law that punishes parents the same regardless of whether death or injury occurs. Until Massachusetts strengthens its civil liability to meet the stricter criminal liability standard recently enacted by the legislature, parents and teenagers will continue to abuse underage drinking without paying a sufficient price. Parents owe a duty not only to their children and their children's friends, but also to innocent third parties, not to allow teenagers to drink at all. If the courts fail to recognize this, the party will continue well into the night. . . .

Development of Social Host Liability in the United States

The development of social host liability in the United States is consistently rooted in modern tort law and relies primarily on negligence principles. At early common law, for example, an individual who furnished alcohol to an intoxicated guest at his home was not held liable for any subsequent injuries because it was thought that the drinking of the alcohol, and not its procurement, was the proximate cause of the injury. With increasing drunk-driving related fatalities, however, this position gradually lost favor and many legislatures enacted dram-shop [an establishment serving alcoholic beverages] laws and other statutes that allowed a cause of action to be brought against liquor vendors or bar owners so that responsibility could be attributed somewhere. Historically, though, these same legislatures were reluctant to impose similar duties on social hosts because they believed that individuals serving drinks to guests in their homes were not in the same position as bartenders; nor did they possess the same experience to determine when a guest had consumed too much alcohol and, consequently, became a threat to third parties. Overwhelming policy considerations eventually forced a change in that school of thought as well.

In 1984, the New Jersey Supreme Court decided the seminal case of *Kelly v. Gwinnell*, laying out a common-law standard of social host liability that is still precedent today. At issue before the court was whether a social host who served a visibly intoxicated adult guest at his home owed a duty to the victim of an automobile accident later caused by that drunken guest. The superior court had originally granted summary judgment in favor of the host, reasoning that New Jersey had never extended

PARENTS' RESPONSIBILITY FOR TEEN DRINKING

Should parents be held responsible for teen drinking at their house, even if they didn't condone it?

No
46%

Yes
54%

Total number of votes: 11,570

Taken from: Kavita Varma-White, "Are Parents Responsible for Teen Drinking, Even If They Don't Know About It?," *TODAYMoms* blog, December 7, 2011. (Live poll as of February 21, 2012.) http://moms.today.com.

common law liability to a social host when the guest was not a minor. On appeal, however, the state supreme court decided that prevalent social policy demanded a change and expanded common law liability to include such social hosts.

The court's balancing of public policy and fairness was instrumental to this decision. Though there was little question that all of the elements required for a negligence cause of action were satisfied in the case, the court needed to decide if it was fair to impose a duty on a social host to monitor the intake of alcohol among his guests in order to protect unknown third parties. Abandoning the once prevalent belief that the possibility of litigation should not intrude upon friends gathering at homes for a social drink, the court answered its inquiry by looking heavily into public policy. Citing the growing number of intolerable deaths caused by drunk-driving accidents each year, the historical prohibition of liquor vendors from serving intoxicated patrons, and recently strengthened criminal sanctions against drunk drivers, the court concluded that it was both fair and desirable to impose such a duty on social hosts, thereby creating a cause of action for common law negligence. Since that decision, however, there has been little consanguinity among jurisdictions with regard to social host liability in the United States. . . .

States' Positions on Social Host Liability

Along with Massachusetts, every other state has grappled with the complexities of social host liability and its role in solving underage drinking. Some jurisdictions, for example, view a criminal statutory violation of providing liquor to a minor as proof of negligence or negligence per se when attaching liability to social hosts. Other states simply treat the service of alcohol to minors as a breach of a common-law duty by itself. Others have enacted statutes that permit common-law claims to be brought against social hosts who knowingly furnish alcohol to minors. Conversely, there are states that completely refuse to recognize a duty to prevent alcohol from reaching the hands, or mouths, of minors. Regardless of the approach, underage drinking is a country-wide problem that needs to be addressed seriously by courts and legislatures.

States that have not recognized social host liability have hedged on the issue because of an understanding that it is the responsibility of the legislature, not the courts, to create a new cause of action. Rhode Island courts, for example, currently do not recognize social host liability simply because the government has never expressly told them that they could do so. Additionally, these states are reluctant to impose a common-law duty on hosts to monitor alcohol use among minors, where no such common-law duty exists for adult guests because they feel that there is no rational distinction between the two.

The states that do attach social host liability to adults for providing alcohol to minors usually do so through common-law negligence principles or statutory violations. An abundance of states, for example, view underage drinkers as a special class that legislatures have specifically sought to protect from the dangers of alcohol through the enactment of various liquor laws and criminal sanctions. When a parent or adult violates one of those statutes, it is proof that they have acted unreasonably, resulting in negligence per se. Other states, however, do not believe that such a statute is necessary to conclude that handing liquor to an underage drinker is unreasonable or that doing so causes foreseeable risks to both the minor and innocent third parties. These states simply impose a common-law duty on adults to refrain from acting unreasonably in their distribution of alcohol to minors.

Finally, there are states that enact statutes specifically prohibiting hosts from providing alcohol to underage drinkers. Minnesota, for example, allows common-law tort claims to be brought by anyone injured by an intoxicated minor, though the host may use the defense of contributory negligence to limit his liability. The legislature, through enactment of this statute, has sought to place social hosts on the same footing as commercial vendors, expanding liability to effectively deter underage drinking in the state. Additionally, Minnesota has passed a keg registration law that acts as an investigative tool to determine who actually provided alcohol to minor drinkers in order to pursue civil damages claims against a host. Parents, then, must think twice about providing alcohol to underage drinkers in their homes as they are vulnerable to both heavy civil and criminal penalties. . . .

Some critics argue that it is the parents' responsibility to educate their children about drinking and to monitor alcohol use in their homes. Therefore, they say, parents should be liable for injuries to other parties caused by drinking and driving. © Image Source/Corbis.

Problems with Treating Minors as Adults for Social Host Liability

Most troubling about the current state of social host liability law in Massachusetts is the court's identical treatment of adult and underage drinking guests. The rule established in *McGuiggan v. New England Telephone and Telegraph Co.*, for example, makes a social host liable only when he knows or should have known that his guest was drunk but continued to serve him alcohol anyway. The standard is based on common-law principles of negligence where the host breached a duty by creating a reasonably foreseeable risk to third parties who might later come into contact with the inebriated guest. If the guests serve themselves, however, the duty disappears because it is not the conduct of the social host that created the risk of injury to third parties. While the standard is sensible when applied to adults, it loses its practicality with regard to underage drinkers.

Minors under the age of twenty-one are a special class of society, recognized by the legislature as needing extra protection from the many harms of alcohol. Parents who allow minors to drink, then, are culpable enough to be committing a crime but not negligent enough to create a duty to protect third parties from foreseeable harm. Presumably, this is because parents that do not actually serve alcohol to the underage guests are in no position to tell whether or not they are drunk, in accordance with the *McGuiggan* standard. This is where the law fails, however, because drunkenness is essentially the equivalent of consuming an excessive amount of alcohol. While a more seasoned adult drinker may consume multiple beverages before he has drunk to excess, making it difficult for a host to determine intoxication, every drop of liquor illegally consumed by a minor is excessive. A reasonable host should recognize that making any amount of alcohol available to minors, even indirectly, will result in drunk guests and, consequently, the foreseeable harm that the legislature had hoped to prevent by restricting the drinking age to twenty-one.

The court's logic also fails in its view that the underage guest, as opposed to the adult host, is in the best position to prevent injury to himself. In its continuing effort to achieve uniformity in its decisions regardless of the age of the social guest involved, the court disregards common sense much like the parents who host underage drinking parties. It is easy to recognize, for example, that an underage drinker who has had almost no experience with the dangerous effects of alcohol is incapable of deciding for himself at what point he has had enough to drink. Indeed, the minor has actually had too much when he consumes his first drop, making it even more unreasonable for the parent to allow consumption until the minor sees fit to stop. It is troubling, then, that parents allow teenagers to make this determination with full support of the courts, even though the legislature has long since removed that decision from the equation with the passage of various pieces of liquor legislation that disallow individuals under the age of twenty-one from consuming alcohol. If a minor cannot make the decision because of his inexperience and immaturity, and the legislature and law enforcement officials have already instructed teens that they are not to drink, it leaves no one, but the parents who allow underage drinking in their homes, to prevent injuries to third parties or guests. Accordingly, because it is ultimately the responsibility of the parents to prevent harm, the doors of civil liability should be swung wide open when parents fail to correctly monitor these parties and injury unfortunately occurs. . . .

Not the Parents' Decision

The purpose of this [viewpoint] is not to suggest that teenagers should completely refrain from alcoholic consumption until they reach the legal drinking age of twenty-one. Indeed, it may be convincingly argued that a minor's first drink and the uncertainties and pressures that come with it are an important part of adolescence and maturity that should be preserved by allowing kids to be kids. The decision to drink, however, should not be made by the parents who allow underage drinking parties to occur in their homes. By providing a "safer" venue that encourages and promotes underage drinking, parents are not only placing their children and others in danger of serious injury, but are also effectively removing any decision-making process that may allow a minor to weigh his options and think twice before drinking to excess.

> "For there to be a substantial step in
> pursuit of the alleged undertaking,
> there must have been some affirmative
> action taken in an attempt to prohibit
> possession and consumption of alcohol."

Parents May Not Be Liable When Minors Drink in Their Homes

The Illinois Supreme Court's Decision

Lloyd A. Karmeier

In 2006, eighteen-year-old Daniel Bell drove drunk after leaving a party at Jonathan Hutsell's family home and crashed, killing himself and his passenger. Jonathan's parents, Jeffrey and Sara Hutsell, were sued in a civil case, Bell v. Hutsell, *for negligence in voluntarily undertaking the duty to prevent underage drinking. However, the Illinois Supreme Court ruled that the Hutsells were not liable. In the following viewpoint, Lloyd A. Karmeier claims that the couple—who informed their son that underage drinking would be monitored and prohibited but did not enforce this rule during the party—did not affirmatively act to prevent minors from drinking by confiscating alcohol, asking teens to leave, or ending the party. In essence, he concludes, because the Hutsells did not*

Lloyd A. Karmeier, Opinion, *Bell v. Hutsell*, Illinois Supreme Court, May 19, 2011.

assert control over Bell or others, they did not undertake a duty to protect them and therefore did not violate that duty. Karmeier is a fifth district justice on the Illinois Supreme Court.

This case arises out of the death of Daniel Bell, age 18, who died in a single-car accident after he had allegedly consumed alcoholic beverages at the residence of defendants in the course of a party organized and hosted by the defendants' son, Jonathan. Plaintiff's second amended complaint implicitly acknowledges that the defendants did not provide alcohol for underage consumption, and in fact alleges that defendants informed Jonathan both that alcohol consumption would not be tolerated and that they would monitor the party to see that underage partygoers did not possess or imbibe alcoholic beverages. Plaintiff alleges, however, that the Hutsells were aware of underage consumption on their premises at prior parties; that their son, Jonathan, had previously pled guilty to underage consumption; that alcohol was brought to the party in question and underage guests drank, excessively, with the Hutsells' knowledge—in some instances in their presence—without objection or consequence; and that Jerry Hutsell "on multiple occasions spoke to a number of underage partygoers who had been drinking alcohol and requested that if they had been drinking at the party not to drive a vehicle when leaving." The complaint states that Daniel Bell drank alcohol "in full and open view of the defendants," and that he later walked to his car, "began driving," and "crashed his car into a tree," resulting in his death.

With respect to plaintiff's theory of a voluntary undertaking, advanced in counts I through III of the complaint, it was alleged generally, without additional factual reference, that defendants "voluntarily undertook the duty" to prohibit underage drinking and possession of alcoholic beverages on their premises and to inspect, monitor, and supervise partygoers under the age of 21 to those ends.

The complaint then recites various respects in which defendants were "negligent," most of which mirror the general allegations of the complaint, without additional factual elaboration, with the exception of a statement in paragraph 50(i) of the complaint, which includes an allegation that defendants were negligent in "failing to comply with their own verbal directions to the party guests to ensure that underage drinking *and driving* thereafter from their home not occur." (Emphasis added.) Language with respect to the preclusion of driving after the party does not appear in any statements attributed to defendants when the alleged voluntary undertaking was communicated to their son. If the allegation is a reference to the complaint's recitation that Jerry Hutsell "on multiple occasions spoke to a number of underage partygoers who had been drinking alcohol and requested that if they had been drinking at the party not to drive a vehicle when leaving," then it inappropriately equates a "request" with "verbal directions" aimed at ensuring compliance. . . .

The Duty of Care

Plaintiff in this case alleges that defendants voluntarily undertook the duty to prevent the underage consumption of alcoholic beverages on their premises and that they negligently performed that duty.

In order to prevail in an action for negligence, the plaintiff must prove that the defendant owed a duty, that the defendant breached that duty, and that defendant's breach was the proximate cause of injury to the plaintiff. Unless a duty is owed, there can be no recovery in tort for negligence. Whether a duty exists is a question of law for the court to decide via *de novo* [anew] review.

Under a voluntary undertaking theory of liability, the duty of care to be imposed upon a defendant is limited to the extent of the undertaking. The theory is narrowly construed. We have looked to the Restatement (Second) of Torts in defining the parameters of liability pursuant to this theory.

The relevant sections of the Restatement, as identified by the plaintiff, provide as follow:

§323. Negligent Performance of Undertaking to Render Services

One who undertakes, gratuitously or for consideration, to render services to another which he should recognize as necessary for the protection of the other's person or things, is subject to liability to the other for physical harm resulting from his failure to exercise reasonable care to perform his undertaking, if:

> (a) his failure to exercise such care increases the risk of such harm, or
>
> (b) the harm is suffered because of the other's reliance upon the undertaking.

§324A. Liability to Third Person for Negligent Performance of Undertaking

One who undertakes, gratuitously or for consideration, to render services to another which he should recognize as necessary for the protection of a third person or his things, is subject to liability to the third person for physical harm resulting from his failure to exercise reasonable care to protect his undertaking, if:

> (a) his failure to exercise reasonable care increases the risk of such harm, or
>
> (b) he has undertaken to perform a duty owed by the other to the third person, or
>
> (c) the harm is suffered because of reliance on the other or the third person upon the undertaking. . . .

Misfeasance and Nonfeasance

According to plaintiff's complaint, on the date of the party the defendants "voluntarily undertook a duty to prohibit their son and his party guests who were under the age of 21 from drinking alcoholic beverages of any kind at their residence" and to that end also undertook to "monitor and supervise . . . to ensure that none

A young man drinks at a private home under adult supervision. Parents may not be liable in all cases for accidents stemming from teens drinking and driving. © Ryan Pierse/Getty Images.

of the party guests who were under the age of 21 would consume alcoholic beverages." The complaint recites that the alleged undertaking was communicated to defendants' son Jonathan, but there is no claim that the defendants' intent was communicated to anyone else. It is alleged that defendants were present, at times, in the portion of their residence where the party was ongoing, and where plaintiff alleges that underage consumption of alcohol was obviously taking place, that defendants witnessed underage possession and consumption of alcohol; yet, they took no actions to prohibit it in furtherance of the aim of their alleged undertaking.

"'By undertaking to act'" a defendant becomes "'subject to a duty with respect to the manner of performance.'" Although the cited sections of the Restatement do not address a situation like this, where there is a narrowly disseminated statement of intent to engage in a course of conduct, the aim of which might be as much the protection of the defendants' perceived legal interests, as the physical welfare of others who are guests on the premises, comments to section 323 of the Restatement (Second) of Torts do address circumstances under which a mere promise, without entering upon performance, might qualify as a sufficient undertaking within the rule stated in that section. There, the distinction between "misfeasance" (negligent performance of a voluntary undertaking, as alleged in *Wakulich* [*v. Mraz*]) and "nonfeasance" (omission to perform a voluntary undertaking) is discussed as it pertains to tort liability. The commentators observe that the "modern law has . . . witnessed a considerable weakening and blurring of the distinction, *in situations where the plaintiff's reliance upon the defendant's promise has resulted in harm to him.*" Decisions of our appellate court have also underscored the necessity of reliance if a defendant is to be held responsible for nonfeasance: "'Under Illinois law, a plaintiff's reliance on the defendant's promise is an independent, essential element in cases of nonfeasance.'"

The alleged recipient's change of position, or lack thereof, may also be a factor affecting duty and liability when an actor terminates services voluntarily undertaken. Comment c of section 323 addresses an actor's ability to terminate services voluntarily undertaken:

> "The fact that the actor gratuitously starts in to aid another does not necessarily require him to continue his services. He is not required to continue them indefinitely, or even until he has done everything in his power to aid and protect the other. The actor may normally abandon his efforts at any time unless, by giving the aid, he has put the other in a worse position than he was in before the actor attempted to aid him." . . .

No Affirmative Action Taken

The facts alleged by plaintiff in this case suggest that defendants expressed an intention to prohibit underage possession and consumption of alcoholic beverages at the party hosted by their son at their residence. Although plaintiff states that *monitoring* the possession and consumption of alcohol at the party was part of the *duty* voluntarily undertaken by defendants, monitoring alone obviously did nothing to ensure "the protection of the other's person," or "the protection of a third person," pursuant to the requisites of sections 323 and 324A of the Restatement. Monitoring was not, as in some of the cases cited by the plaintiff, the duty itself. Given the facts alleged by plaintiff, it was not even a substantial step in the undertaking. Plaintiff alleges that defendants were aware of underage drinking, and took no action. Given these facts, for there to be a substantial step in pursuit of the alleged undertaking, there must have been some affirmative action taken in an attempt to *prohibit* possession and consumption of alcohol, the ultimate objective of the undertaking. No affirmative action is alleged here. Defendants did not attempt to confiscate alcoholic beverages in the possession of underage partygoers; they did not ask offenders to leave; they did not call a halt to the party—they did nothing. In our view, the facts alleged do not support an inference that defendants commenced substantive performance of their intended undertaking; however, even if we were to assume, *arguendo* [for the sake of argument] such an inference could be reasonably drawn, the alleged circumstances indicate the intent to perform was abandoned.

Moreover, even if we were to find sufficient allegations of a duty voluntarily assumed, pursuant to which performance was commenced, the facts alleged do not provide a basis for liability. The factual allegations of plaintiff's complaint do not support an inference that defendants' stated intent and subsequent inaction increased the risk of harm to Daniel or other partygoers nor does it evince reliance or change of position on the basis of defendants' expressed intent. According to the facts set forth in plaintiff's complaint, defendants' intention to prohibit underage possession and consumption of alcoholic beverages was expressed only to their son, Jonathan. There is no allegation that Jonathan communicated defendants' intention to anyone else. Thus, there

The General Rule Regarding Parental Liability

The general rule regarding parental liability is that the mere relationship between parent and child does not impose any legal liability on
the parent for the bad acts or carelessness of the child. Rather, parents are held liable only when the child is acting as an agent of the
parent or when some carelessness of the parent made the bad act
possible. Some examples regarding parental liability as an agent
include harm resulting from a car accident caused by the negligence of a child when the child was running an errand for a parent,
or when a parent encourages a child to physically attack another
person. Parents also can be held liable when their own negligence
contributes to a child causing injury to another. For instance, if a
parent serves a child alcohol and then permits the child to drive a
car, the parent may be liable for damages. Thus, for a parent to be
found liable for the behavior of his or her child, the child must be
acting on behalf of the parent or the parent must have made the
harm possible through his or her own carelessness or negligence.

*Robert M. Regoli, John D. Hewitt, and Matt
DeLisi,* Delinquency in Society. *Sudbury, MA:
Jones and Bartlett Publishers, 2010.*

are no facts alleged in the complaint that would support an inference of reliance or change of position on the part of any guests
attending the party or, for that matter, any "other" person owing
them some unarticulated, undefined duty. Plaintiff's undevel-
oped suggestion that Jonathan might be the "other" for purposes
of section 324(b) liability fails to account for the fact that the
extent of Jonathan's innate liability to the guests—having undertaken no additional duty—is no greater than any other host in
this situation. He owed Daniel no duty to prevent Daniel's possession or consumption of alcohol.

No Duty Owed

Because defendants in this case took no affirmative acts to effect the aim of their expressed intention, *i.e.*, prohibition, and no one changed position as a result of their statement, relied upon it, or was put at "increase[d] . . . risk of . . . harm" or "in a worse position" because of it, the factual allegations of this case do not support a basis for finding a duty undertaken or liability for violation of any such duty. Indeed, under these circumstances, it would be illogical, and unsound policy, to hold that defendants could be liable: illogical, because defendants' failure to act on their stated intention did not in any way affect the events as they would have unfolded had the intent to act not been verbalized; unsound policy, because the imposition of a duty and liability in this situation would only serve as a deterrent to those who would consider volunteering assistance to others, in effect punishing people for thinking out loud. At most, the allegations of plaintiff's complaint suggest that defendants failed to follow through on an expressed intent to act that *might* have protected Daniel—who was legally underage for the consumption of alcohol, but an adult for most other purposes—against his own volitional acts, or that defendants simply abandoned their original undertaking, whether it was intended for their own protection from the perceived potential of liability, or a genuine concern for the safety of Daniel and other partygoers. We conclude the allegations of plaintiff's complaint are insufficient to state a legal duty and a basis for liability on the part of defendants under either section 323 or 324A of the Restatement.

We note that the facts alleged in this case bear little similarity to those this court addressed in *Wakulich* and *Simmons v. Homatas*, (2010) (employees of club ejected highly intoxicated individual, placed him in his vehicle, and directed him to drive away), both of which were discussed in the parties' briefs to a greater or lesser extent for diverse reasons. In those cases, this court applied Restatement principles, as we have done here. However, in each of those cases defendants' affirmative conduct, amounting to an assertion of control over an inebriated and significantly impaired person, increased the risk of harm to that person and/or created a risk of harm to others. Thus, different considerations applied. Here, where defendants owed Daniel no duty to prohibit his voluntary possession or consumption of alcohol, and took no action to do so pursuant to their verbalized intent, which was communicated only to their son, we have a case of true nonfeasance.

> *"This story may have ended differently*
> *if more parents and adults understood*
> *the consequences of underage drinking."*

A Family Member Discusses the Death of a Relative Due to Underage Drinking and Driving

Personal Narrative

Susanne Sanstra

In the following viewpoint, Susanne Sanstra recounts the tragic death of her sister's husband, who was killed by a drunk teen driver. She describes the painful moment her sister, who was a passenger in the car and survived the crash, revealed to her two young children that their father had died. Sanstra also expresses outrage at finding out that the teen driver was intoxicated and attended a party with hundreds of drinking minors and an adult present. In her opinion, underage alcohol consumption is dangerous in any circumstance, and Sanstra urges adults and parents never to facilitate or allow it. Sanstra is a novelist and screenwriter based in Denver, Colorado.

As all bad news comes, the call came at 4:00 in the morning, January 15th, 2006. "There's been an accident. Lisa is okay, they took her to Memorial Hospital in Colorado Springs. We can't find Steve. He was hurt bad, they can't tell me where he was taken." This was my mom relaying the only information she had about her daughter and the man that had loved her for 15 years. They couldn't tell us where he was taken because he was never taken to a hospital. He was taken directly to the morgue.

He was killed instantly when a 16-year-old kid that had been drinking drove across the centerline on Highway 83 and ran head on into the car that Steve was driving. Lisa was in the backseat and had to kick out a window to get out of the car. Steve's friend since childhood . . . was in the front seat passenger side. He had broken bones and was bleeding profusely. Lisa stayed with [him] until help arrived, reaching across him to hold her husband's hand and praying, constantly praying.

The next morning I was at Lisa's side in her hospital bed as she told her two small boys that their father had been killed in a terrible car accident. I have never in my life experienced anything so hard, so sad. At the same time, I was so proud of my sister. She was incredible, she cried with them and kept telling them that she was going to take care of them, that they would be okay. She managed to reassure them in the worst moment of their lives. We all cried through their heart piercing wails. The 9-year-old really understood that he would never see his dad again but I think the 6-year-old was confused and cried mostly because the moment was so scary.

This was all 6 months ago. We have had some really bad moments since. Both personal moments that come from losing someone that was a central part of our lives, and moments that revolve around the night of the accident. We found out days after the accident that the boy that hit them was drunk. Next we found out that there had been a huge barn party with hundreds of kids drinking and an adult at the party. That adult was arrested this week with a felony charge of contributing to the delinquency of minors. He bonded out the next day.

The Problem with Accepting Underage Drinking

I am writing this story because I am outraged. There were a hundred teenagers at that party. They were drinking alcohol and smoking pot. This adult at the party was with the kids drinking at the beginning of the party and then came back to kick them out of the barn at 1 AM. Where are all the parents of those kids? Why were they not more aware of where their kids were and why aren't they as outraged as I am? Any one of those teenagers could have been involved in this accident. Any one of them could have killed another person or themselves. Everyone in this community should be aware of this case and should be aware of the problem involving underage drinking.

Since this accident we have heard from too many people, adults and parents both, who think that underage drinking is not the problem. They believe that if they control the situation when kids are drinking and instill the idea that they never drive when drinking then there will be no problem. Obviously that is not true. The problem with accepting underage drinking is once you give them the idea that it is okay they will do it in any situation. In this situation an adult that was not accepting any responsibility for the kids was involved. He kicked them out, drunk or not, and made them all drive away. My brother-in-law was killed moments afterward.

I want to end this story by telling you about Steve. He loved my sister. That is the most honest and important thing I can say about him. He adored her. She knew it. He loved his children. He was a great dad! He was involved in their lives. He coached soccer and was a Boy Scout leader. He was always there for everyone and touched many lives. He was important to us, to his wife, Lisa, and his children. He is greatly missed; our hearts and lives will never be the same. This story may have ended differently it more parents and adults understood the consequences of underage drinking. The only answer is to never allow it, and certainly not to ever contribute

| "Strictly prohibit sales to minors, providing few if any exceptions."

Regulations Prohibiting the Sale of Alcohol to Minors Should Be Strictly Enforced

Deborah A. Fisher

In the following viewpoint, Deborah A. Fisher recommends that the sale and commercial availability of alcohol to minors be more tightly restricted. In her view, states and localities must enact the following regulations on the sale of alcohol: prohibit sales to minors with no or very few exceptions; crack down on commercial outlets that are common sites for underage purchases; place into effect serving and selling practices that reduce underage alcohol sales; launch programs to ensure retailers comply with laws; and enforce administrative, criminal, and civil penalties for offenses. Fisher is a research scientist for the Alcohol, Policy, and Safety Research Center at the Pacific Institute for Research and Evaluation in Calverton, Maryland.

Deborah A. Fisher, "Regulatory Strategies for Preventing Youth Access to Alcohol: Best Practices," Office of Juvenile Justice and Delinquency Prevention, US Department of Justice, April 2000, pp. 5–12.

Commercial availability is shaped by State and local regulations, which determine the number, location, types, and serving and selling practices of alcohol retailers. Great variation is evident in how States regulate commercial availability. Some States are very restrictive and may stipulate State ownership of off-sale outlets, limited number and types of outlets, and local prohibition (in "local-option States"), while other States have only limited controls.

All 50 States prohibit sales to those under age 21, although definitions of "sales" and possible exceptions differ among jurisdictions. The overall structure of alcohol availability in a particular locale will influence the effectiveness of the prohibition. For example, young people have reported that some outlets, notably convenience stores, are more likely than others to sell to minors. In at least one compliance check report, geographic areas with a high density of retailers and low per capita income have lower rates of compliance with underage purchase laws.

Thus, States and localities need to address the following five sets of commercial sales regulations:

1. Strictly prohibit sales to minors, providing few if any exceptions;
2. Limit the types and locations of commercial outlets that are likely sites for youth purchases;
3. Mandate serving and selling practices that reduce the likelihood of illegal sales to minors;
4. Conduct comprehensive compliance check enforcement programs; and
5. Impose appropriate administrative, criminal, and civil penalties for violations.

Strict Prohibitions of Sales or Gifts to Minors

Although all States prohibit alcohol sales to minors, some States permit exceptions. For example, in several States, minors can legally obtain alcohol from a commercial vendor if they are accompanied by a parent or guardian, or they can purchase and deliver alcohol to parents if they have a written authorization. These exceptions further complicate the role and duty of the commercial server in determining who may legally purchase alcohol. If an exception is desired allowing parents or spouses to provide alcohol to minors, it should at least be limited to private residences. The best practice is to prohibit *all* commercial transactions (including sales and gifts) to those under age 21, as is the practice in most States. As a matter of fairness, commercial vendors should have an affirmative defense that they reasonably or in good faith relied on apparently valid, yet false, identification.

Licensing Restrictions

Restricting the location of retail outlets. Many States and local governments create geographic buffer zones between alcohol outlets and schools, playgrounds, other youth facilities, and residential neighborhoods. Distance requirements vary widely—they may apply to only certain types of outlets, and the restrictions may be discretionary by either the State or local licensing body and applicable only if the school administration files a protest.

Most States give local jurisdictions discretion to create buffer zones using local land use and zoning ordinances, a strategy that many cities are now using.

Youth buffer zones create a barrier between young people and alcohol and have both practical and symbolic benefits. By reducing the number of alcohol outlets that are readily accessible, they make it more difficult for young people to purchase alcohol. In many communities, buffer zones will also reduce the number of convenience stores in residential areas. This may be particularly important near schools, limiting the possibility of student consumption during and after school. They also send a community message that alcohol and young people are not a good mix. To be effective, buffer zones require a large enough geographic area and permit only limited exceptions.

Restricting special licenses from youth- or family-oriented community events. States and/or local governments typically issue special, temporary licenses for alcohol sales at special events such as music concerts, community fairs and celebrations, and sporting events. Some venues, such as sporting arenas or concert halls, may receive a special events license that permits ongoing sales on the premises and is not limited to a specific event. Criteria for special events licenses vary, although in most jurisdictions they are readily available at low cost with few restrictions. Licensees may be nonprofit organizations that use alcohol sales as a fundraising strategy. In some cases, the alcohol sales are linked to an alcohol company's sponsorship of the event. In exchange for funding, event organizers agree to sell the company's products and publicize the company's sponsorship.

Alcohol sales at community events create a high risk of underage drinking and related problems, including assaults, drinking and driving, and vandalism. States and local jurisdictions have taken various steps to reduce these risks, including:

- Restricting the issuance of licenses at youth-oriented and family events;
- Prohibiting alcohol sales at specific venues popular with young people;
- Designating alcohol-free days or periods within longer events such as community fairs;
- Establishing restricted drinking sections at special events where young people are not permitted to enter;
- Prohibiting participants from bringing alcohol into the event; and
- Requiring responsible beverage service management policies and training.

A clerk at a liquor store in Massachusetts uses a scanner to verify IDs. Advances in technology make it easier for businesses to verify that a buyer is of legal age. © Darren McCollester/Getty Images.

Strong market and political forces often oppose such regulations. A decision to ban alcohol sales may threaten an alcohol company's sponsorship of the event. Many politically connected nonprofit organizations are dependent on alcohol sales at special events, and alcohol sales are viewed by many special event planners as an integral, lucrative component. These economic and political forces may deter governmental action. For example, the city council in Greenwood, Mississippi, concerned that a ban would hurt the local economy, rejected a citizen drive to ban beer sales at festivals and events held on city property. Despite this type of resistance, many communities are successfully imposing new restrictions on such sales.

States and communities should review and reform their licensing practices for special events. Regulations should strictly limit alcohol sales and alcohol company sponsorships at youth- and family-oriented events, reviewing each on a case-by-case basis. If a special license is issued, alcohol should be incidental to the purpose of the event, and strict policies should ensure that sales to young people do not occur. These policies should include requirements that the organizer create a designated, cordoned-off area for alcohol sales and consumption where young people are not allowed, and provide adequate training to staff and security. Nonprofit organizations should be permitted a limited number of special licenses in a year. . . .

Some communities use methods other than designating a cordoned-off area to prevent sales to minors at community events. These include issuing wristbands to people over 21 to indicate that they can buy alcohol. Such strategies are easily subverted. Restricting access to the area where alcohol is sold is the most effective means of reducing access to alcohol by minors at community events.

Regulations for Serving and Selling Practices

Age of server and seller. States impose varying limits on the minimum age of employees working in commercial alcohol outlets, with many States distinguishing between those who serve alcohol (e.g., bartenders and waitresses in on-premise establishments) and those who sell it (e.g., clerks in off-premise establishments). Virginia and North Carolina impose no age limit for off-premise employees but set a minimum age of 18 (Virginia) and 21 (North Carolina) for alcohol servers.

Minimum ages vary from 16 to 21 years of age in other States, with the large majority designating 18 as the minimum age for either sales or service. Some States, including California, allow 18-year-olds to sell alcohol, provided they are continuously supervised by someone over age 21. Other States distinguish between bartenders and grocery store employees. In most States, the age limits do not apply to employees who are not engaged in selling or serving alcohol. . . .

Restrictions on minors' access to public drinking establishments. State and local regulations vary widely in the extent to which they permit minors to enter on-sale retail alcohol outlets. Most States restrict minors' access to bars and nightclubs and allow them to enter restaurants, and some States prohibit minors from entering any licensed establishment. If the distinction between a bar and a restaurant is blurred, problems can result. California law, for example, permits minors to enter licensed restaurants, but restaurants are required only to have the *capacity* to serve meals, and many maintain bars on the premises and function more as nightclubs, particularly late at night.

Allowing minors into drinking establishments such as bars and nightclubs is, in the words of one enforcement official, "a regulator's nightmare." It creates numerous difficulties for servers, who must conduct repeated identification checks and continuously track who is actually drinking the beverages being served. If minors are barred from the establishment, age identification checks can occur primarily at the door, conducted by a trained employee using proper tools and lighting, thus greatly reducing the ability of minors to obtain alcohol on the premises. The restaurant exception should be applied only to bona fide restaurants that provide table service, maintain a high ratio of food to alcohol sales, and do not have a separate bar or drinking section accessible to minors.

Easy detection of false identification. Many minors possess false identification that they may use in attempts to purchase alcoholic beverages. Research suggests that, in most instances, young people do not need to use false identification because so many retailers in a community routinely sell to them without asking for proof of age. False identification still contributes to youth access, however, and State and local governments and retailers can take two relatively simple steps to reduce its use.

First, several States have redesigned State drivers licenses and identification cards to make them tamper-proof and easy to examine. California and other States, for example, issue minors' licenses and cards with profile photographs and use plastic materials that are difficult to alter. Second, States can require that licensed outlets install and use State drivers license scanners. The scanner reads the magnetic strip on the back of the license so that the user can determine the validity of the birth date and other identifying information printed on the front. Pennsylvania is the first State to introduce scanners at retail outlets. Stores in the State have now installed them, and the State is making them available to alcohol retailers for $900. Seven-Eleven stores in California have installed similar devices. This new technology, combined with changes in license and identification card design, provides valuable tools for retailers to reduce the risk of accepting invalid identification from minors attempting to purchase alcohol.

Home delivery and Internet sales. Only one study has been conducted to date on youth access through home delivery. This practice (legal in about half the States) allows off-sale retailers to deliver alcohol to the purchaser at a private residence. The researchers surveyed young people and retailers in 15 small and midsize communities in Minnesota and Wisconsin. Their findings are startling: 10 percent of 12th graders and 7.3 percent of 18- to 20-year-olds reported purchasing alcohol delivered by a retailer to a home or individual in the past year. The authors speculate that high school seniors are more likely to use delivery services because their older counterparts can easily access alcohol by other means. Those using this method are also more likely to engage in heavy, high-risk drinking, and retailers who engage in home delivery are more likely to sell beer kegs.

As these findings suggest, home deliveries open an additional avenue for youth access to alcohol. Delivery personnel are not monitored by management, surveillance cameras, or law enforcement, so they may be less likely to inspect identification; and young people may also feel less risk of exposure or penalties for these purchases. If asked for identification, they can simply say the person ordering the alcohol is not present. Home delivery may also be one means to supply teen parties in private residences, which often involve large quantities of alcohol, including kegs. For these reasons, at least one community coalition has sought strict control of home deliveries of alcohol.

Internet and mail-order sales raise similar concerns, and there have been numerous reports of shippers leaving alcohol addressed to children at private residences. Controls are even less likely in these cases, since the deliveries are being made by firms whose normal business is not alcohol sales, thereby making them less familiar with legal requirements regarding underage sales and proper identification. No research has been published on the prevalence of young people ordering alcohol through the Internet or by mail order, however, and the risk appears smaller than that for home delivery for at least three reasons: (1) this method of purchase takes a long time (at least a week in most cases); (2) credit cards are usually required; and (3) the products being offered are more likely to be expensive.

Internet and mail-order sales have stimulated a contentious political battle, however, not only because they might increase access to minors but also because State tax agencies are concerned about lost tax revenues, and alcohol wholesalers are concerned that their markets may be undermined. The wholesalers have joined with several organizations including public health groups to form Americans for Responsible Alcohol Access (ARAA). This new coalition seeks to prohibit Internet/mail-order alcohol sales, arguing that they increase alcohol access to minors. Small wineries, which oppose regulation, argue that restrictions violate their constitutional rights under the interstate

"Problems with underage drinking?" Copyright © 1994, Jim Huber. Reproduced by permission.

commerce clause. They also contend that wholesalers are seeking controls not because of risks of selling to minors but because they want to maintain a monopoly on all alcohol distribution in their territories. Congress and many State legislatures are now grappling with these conflicting economic, interstate commerce, and health agendas.

If States permit either home delivery or Internet/mail-order sales, they can reduce the risk of youth access by establishing strict procedures similar to those used in beer keg sales. As a condition of sale, the deliverer should be required to fill out a form that includes the amount of alcohol being purchased, the purchaser's drivers license or State identification card number, and an affidavit signed by the purchaser confirming that he or she is at least age 21 and understands the civil and criminal penalties for furnishing alcohol to minors. The deliverer should be required to maintain these files for a set period of time and produce them to enforcement agencies on demand; failure to maintain records should result in administrative penalties. The purchaser can similarly be held liable both criminally and civilly if he or she furnishes the alcohol to minors.

Mandated responsible beverage service programs. Responsible beverage service programs target both on-sale and off-sale alcohol retailers and are designed to reduce sales to minors and intoxicated adults. They include three critical components:

1. Policy development,
2. Manager training, and
3. Server/seller training.

Evaluations of their effectiveness (which have focused primarily on preventing intoxication) are mixed but promising. In general, programs are more likely to be successful when they include a policy development component, focus on skills development and active learning, and are implemented communitywide in conjunction with compliance checks and a media advocacy campaign. Compliance checks may be particularly important to ensure success of the underage sales component. Evaluations of merchant education programs targeting tobacco sales to minors have reached similar conclusions. Two studies suggest that mandated responsible beverage service programs that require all establishments in a jurisdiction to participate are more effective than programs implemented on a voluntary basis. Mandated programs may not be politically or practically feasible, however, until after a community or State has developed and implemented voluntary programs. . . .

Unfortunately, research findings have not played a major role in this implementation process. Most programs focus primarily on server training and ignore policy development and manager training. Often they lack a community component. In some cases they are instituted by industry groups as an alternative to, instead of in conjunction with, compliance checks and other policy interventions. In such cases, responsible beverage service programs are at best doing no harm.

Responsible beverage service programs focus primarily on sales to intoxicated persons but include a component on preventing sales to minors. A comprehensive curriculum will ensure adoption and implementation of the following policies (on a voluntary basis, if not mandated by the local or State jurisdiction):

- Minimum age of 21 for servers and sellers;
- Staff notification and acknowledgment of legal responsibility and consequences for violation;
- Procedures to ensure that all persons seeking entry or service will be subject to an identification check (including denying entry to bar areas);
- Identification checks for anyone who appears to be age 30 or younger (higher ages in some circumstances);
- Guidelines regarding acceptable identification cards and procedures for establishing validity; and
- Internal compliance checks conducted by management to ensure compliance.

The manager and server training components focus on implementation of these policies, using active learning techniques. The training should emphasize management policies that are likely to lead to more responsible practices.

The Importance of Compliance Checks

Routine, comprehensive compliance checks are the key strategy for deterring commercial alcohol sales to minors. They involve the use of underage buyers by law enforcement agencies as deputies to test retailers' compliance with laws regarding the sale of alcohol to minors. A comprehensive program consists of the following components:

- Notification to retailers, including the program's goals, procedures, and timeframes;
- Opportunity for retailers to participate in responsible sales and service programs prior to the start of the compliance check;
- Community outreach and media advocacy to publicize the program's design and purpose;
- Random selection of outlets to be included in the initial wave of the program (100-percent coverage if feasible);
- Follow-up communication informing each retailer of the results; and
- Repeated notifications to licensees of the ongoing compliance check program and repeated waves of checks over set periods of time (two or more times per year), which may include targeted checks of retailers identified as violators in previous waves.

> *"The combination of incentive and reward offered by the education and licensing program promises positive effects for those under and over 18 alike."*

A Graduated Alcohol Licensing System for Ages Eighteen to Twenty Should Be Established

Choose Responsibility

In the following viewpoint, Choose Responsibility proposes that a graduated alcohol licensing system for eighteen- to twenty-year-olds would help eliminate the widespread problems of clandestine alcohol consumption and binge drinking among youth. The organization explains that the licensing system would require alcohol consumption under the supervision of a parent or guardian and the completion of an alcohol-education course teaching moderation and responsibility. Additionally, Choose Responsibility continues, violations such as furnishing alcohol to minors or drinking before age eighteen would result in the postponement of drinking privileges. Founded by John M. McCardell Jr., president emeritus of Middlebury College, Choose Responsibility is a nonprofit orga-

nization that advocates lowering the minimum drinking age of twenty-one.

If the drinking age is lowered, what provisions could be made to keep alcohol from being readily available to those younger than 18?

In order to act as functional social policy, any attempt to lower the drinking age would need to be accompanied by provisions intended to keep alcohol away from young people under 18. Instead of lowering the drinking age to 18 and automatically allowing 18 year-olds all the privileges enjoyed now by those 21 and older, a better approach may be to regulate alcohol use by those 18–20 years of age through a graduated licensing system. This could consist of a period following an individual's eighteenth birthday in which he or she could drink only under the supervision of a parent or guardian. That individual could then pay a fee reflective of the program's implementation cost and enroll in a state-administered alcohol education course. Upon successful completion of the course requirements, an alcohol license would be issued, allowing that individual to consume alcohol within the confines of the law.

In order to prevent minors' ease of access to alcohol, anyone who chooses to enroll in the course must have successfully completed secondary education. Furthermore, anyone with an alcohol license who is caught driving while intoxicated, furnishing alcohol to minors, or in violation of any other provision of the law would have his or her license and all drinking privileges revoked until reaching age 21.

A Successful Model for Responsible and Moderate Behavior
What might an alcohol education program look like?

Since there is no comprehensive course that fits the needs of an education program of this magnitude, the recommended alcohol

John McCardell testifies before the Vermont legislature in 2010. Choose Responsibility, the group he founded, argues that states should be allowed to lower the drinking age. © AP Images/Toby Talbot.

education course would be an amalgam of effective programs presently available, designed by alcohol experts and educators. Learning to drive a vehicle and learning to drink responsibly are remarkably similar processes; accordingly, we believe that an alcohol education course modeled on the length and format of driver's education has much to recommend it. We envision a course comprised of both inside- and outside-the-classroom sessions that culminate in a final examination whose successful completion earns the student a license to purchase and consume alcohol. Course content would include a detailed review of alcohol laws, the history of alcohol use in America, information regarding the short- and long-term effects of alcohol on the body and brain, how America's beliefs about alcohol use compare to those of the rest of the world, and explanations of what is responsible drinking versus irresponsible drinking. Ultimately, the primary goal of the course is to reinforce responsible drinking and encourage young adults to make informed decisions about alcohol use. The available literature suggests that the best way to do this is through social norms education, a practice that informs the individual of actual rates of alcohol use among his or her peers—numbers which are often much lower than expected. This has been shown to have the effect of reducing consumption and harmful drinking patterns. An alcohol education course would also provide a forum for various views in the community, hopefully including local MADD [Mothers Against Drunk Driving] chapters, law enforcement, and public health officials. These groups would play a role both in the development of the course modules and by involving students in outside-the-classroom sessions, such as experiencing court hearings in drunken driving cases or attending a meeting of a local alcoholics' support group.

Why would a mandatory alcohol education course have the effect of decreasing irresponsible drinking and other problematic, alcohol-related behaviors?

If developed and implemented correctly, a mandatory alcohol education course would present new drinkers with a successful model for responsible and moderate behavior. By avoiding the pitfalls encountered by previous alcohol education programs— especially those that stress complete abstinence, the costs incurred as a result of alcohol-related crime and accidents, or the negative and addictive qualities of alcohol—such a program could define and model responsible use. Instead of highlighting the negative consequences of consumption and stigmatizing any and all alcohol use, an effective program would provide guidelines for healthy ways to consume alcohol, discourage drinking to the point of intoxication, and clearly outline both the negative and positive social and personal effects of drinking. The program would also be accompanied by a clear presentation of drinking laws and penalties for their violation. Provided to all newly enfranchised drinkers, the course information would present a viable, socially acceptable alternative to binge and goal-oriented drinking—the two activities that lead most often to auto accidents, crime, and overdose.

Above and beyond the content of the course, the effectiveness of an alcohol education program is contingent upon treating its subjects as adults. The existence of such a course would serve as acknowledgement of the fact that those over 18 can make healthy, informed decisions when armed with the right information. For many adolescents, alcohol is a vehicle for social rebellion, its abuse a function of asserting one's independence from infantilizing social policies. An alcohol education course would help normalize society's treatment of alcohol and its users.

A Better Option than the Current Legal Drinking Age
Why would a lowered drinking age work better than Legal Age 21?

There is overwhelming evidence which shows that the vast majority of 18–20 year olds choose to ignore the law and drink anyway. Unfortunately, since these young adults are breaking the law, they choose to drink in clandestine locations to avoid prosecution. This promotes unsafe and irresponsible drinking and has led to the development of a dangerous subculture among today's youth defined by drinking games, "pregaming," and large, out-of-control parties whose sole focus is drinking beyond the point of intoxication.

Should the legal drinking age be lowered to 18, the privilege to drink would be contingent upon completion of an intensive alcohol education course specifically aimed at reducing at-risk drinking and promoting responsible, safe consumption. Because young adults would no longer have to drink behind closed doors to avoid getting caught, their formative encounters with alcohol would be in supervised, controlled environments. An 18-year-old drinking age would effectively remove young adults' drinking from secretive, and dangerous locations.

If you can't keep alcohol from passing between college seniors to freshmen, what makes you think that there would be any greater success in stopping this transfer from 18 year-olds to younger teenagers?

A graduated licensing system has the potential to restrict the transfer of alcohol from 18-year-olds to younger teens. After a period of being permitted to drink only under parental supervision, 18-year-olds would then be allowed to enroll in an extensive alcohol education course, earning a drinking license upon successful completion. Individuals would be prevented from enrolling in the course until finishing secondary education.

Furthermore, any violation of the state's alcohol control laws, such as furnishing to minors or driving under the influence of alcohol, would result in immediate suspension of the drinking license. Young people caught drinking before they reach age 18 and obtain a license would be delayed from enrolling in the alcohol education course for a specified period of time.

"Blood Borders" and the Loss of Federal Highway Funding

If a state were to implement an 18 year-old drinking age, how would you keep its borders from becoming "blood borders?"

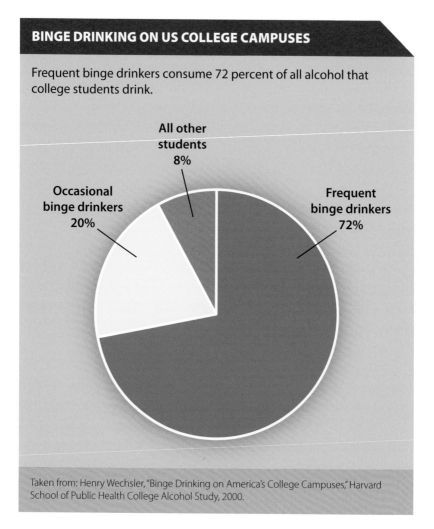

BINGE DRINKING ON US COLLEGE CAMPUSES

Frequent binge drinkers consume 72 percent of all alcohol that college students drink.

All other students
8%

Occasional binge drinkers
20%

Frequent binge drinkers
72%

Taken from: Henry Wechsler, "Binge Drinking on America's College Campuses," Harvard School of Public Health College Alcohol Study, 2000.

Because alcohol use by 18–20-year-olds would be permitted only with an appropriate license, it would be illegal for residents between those ages who live in neighboring states to enter that state and purchase alcohol. The privilege to obtain such a license would be limited to that state's residents and full-time students at its residential colleges. If necessary, an electronic scanning system could provide a sufficient technological deterrent to counterfeiting, and improve ID-checking protocols in liquor outlets, grocery stores, bars, and restaurants.

If my state lowers its drinking age, it will just lose millions of dollars each year in federal highway funding. What will this proposal do to remedy that?

We acknowledge that little change can take place on the state level so long as the federal government threatens to withhold a substantial amount of highway funding each year. Accordingly, a major part of our proposal is to recommend that Congress permit states to apply for a waiver of the federal highway-funding condition. In order to obtain such a waiver, states that hope to lower the drinking age must submit to Congress a coherent and comprehensive plan to educate and license young adults to purchase, possess and consume alcohol. A waiver would only be granted to a state with an acceptable program on the grounds that it must show a measurable decrease in the incidence of alcohol-related traffic crashes and fatalities, as well as in rates of binge drinking and other factors related to harmful drinking. The appropriate data, all of which is already collected and analyzed by various governmental agencies, would be gathered over a five-year period and presented to Congress at its completion. Based on those findings, a state could request an extension of the waiver for another five-year period.

Providing a Safe and Supervised Setting

Why do you think a change in the legal drinking age is a viable strategy for reducing harmful and dangerous drinking patterns in young people?

The combination of incentive and reward offered by the education and licensing program promises positive effects for those under and over 18 alike. Penalties for violation of alcohol control laws will encourage younger adolescents to abstain until they reach age 18; at the same time, those laws will encourage those over 18 who choose to drink to do so responsibly, so as to avoid revocation of their drinking license. Perhaps most importantly, though, this proposal will re-involve parents, teachers, and other role models in the process of teaching young adults how to drink in moderation. Marginalized under the current law, these figures would again be legally permitted to introduce young adults to alcohol consumption in the home and other safe, supervised locations.

Would reducing the drinking age be a recipe for public health disaster?

Advocates of a 21-year-old drinking age claim that lowering the drinking age would lead to several public health problems. Their concerns are twofold: increased rates of alcohol abuse and decreased mental faculties amongst new drinkers.

If the present 21 year-old drinking age were actually effective in reducing underage drinking in the 18–20-year-old cohort, then lowering the drinking age to 18 could very well increase rates of alcohol abuse. The logic is that a lower drinking age would provide access to alcohol to otherwise abstinent but potential abusers. However, the reality of the present drinking age is that it is ineffective in keeping alcohol out of the hands of underage drinkers, specifically those who are already in college, ages 18–20. Albeit misguided, the argument concerning the risk-prone nature of young adults is an important one. If the drinking age were lowered, it would give colleges and universities, and foremost parents, the opportunity to promote the healthy use of alcohol and provide a safe and supervised setting for young adults to consume alcohol. In terms of controlling and forestalling risky behavior, such an environment would be a vast improvement over the basements, dorm rooms, and fraternity houses where risky drinking behavior currently takes place. Secondly, if consuming alcohol before the age of 21 does have a deleterious effect on the cognitive abilities of drinkers should there not be an entire generation of Americans that came of age from 1973–1984, even whole continents of people (Europe, most of Asia, Latin America, and Oceania), who are less intelligent, or cognitively impaired because of their early exposure to alcohol? The premise of such an argument is so outlandish, in fact, that no such study has ever been conducted.

Out of Step with Cultural Attitudes

Why lower the drinking age now when there are more pressing matters facing the country?

In the more than two decades that have passed since its implementation, the 21-year-old drinking age has created a climate in which terms like "binge" and "pregame" have come to describe young peoples' choices about alcohol; in which the law is habitually and thoughtlessly ignored by adolescents and adults alike; in which colleges and communities across the nation are plagued with out-of-control parties, property damage, and belligerent drunks; in which emergency rooms and campus health centers are faced with an alarming number of sometimes fatal cases of alcohol poisoning and overdose on weekend nights; and in which the role of parents in teaching responsible behavior around alcohol has been marginalized and the family disenfranchised. Maintaining status quo in America today is not an option.

We are faced with a law that is out of step with our cultural attitudes towards alcohol, one which encourages violation and breeds disrespect. Historically, we know that during the Vietnam War the 26th Amendment in 1971 provided 18-year-olds the right to vote, the age at which one could be drafted to fight in the war. This constitutional recognition of 18-year-olds as consenting adults was fundamental for guaranteeing the right for 18-year-olds to drink. Again, a quarter century later, we are engaged in a war where many of the soldiers currently serving abroad are under the legal drinking age of 21. And while that historical parallel itself does not provide justification for changing the drinking age, it makes strikingly clear the poor logic behind the assumption that the age of 18 is too immature for alcohol consumption. If the drinking age were lowered, it would signal a transformation in the relationship our society has with its young adults. Besides engendering greater respect for the law, a lower and more easily enforced drinking age would offer alternative choices for parents and college campuses around the country in shaping responsible drinking behaviors and encouraging informed decisions about alcohol use.

> "The Amethyst Initiative says, in essence, that the phenomenon of underage drinking is a tidal wave that society cannot stop."

The Initiative to Loosen Drinking Restrictions for Ages Eighteen to Twenty Is Harmful

Carla T. Main

In the following viewpoint, Carla T. Main asserts that the Amethyst Initiative—which aims to replace the twenty-one-and-over drinking age with alcohol education and regulated consumption for eighteen- to twenty-year-olds—is not the solution to harmful drinking patterns among youths. She argues that binge drinking is not driven by alcohol's illegality or the secrecy of underage drinking, and lowering the minimum age would actually increase excessive consumption. Main also maintains that drinking differs from other rights granted at age eighteen, as youths require protection from the health-altering effects of alcohol. Alcohol education already takes place at many colleges and universities, she says, but such programs have unproven impacts on student drinking rates and habits. A former lawyer, Main writes on legal issues and was associate editor of the National Law Journal. *She is the author of* Bulldozed.

Carla T. Main, "Underage Drinking and the Drinking Age," *Policy Review*, vol. 155, June 1, 2009. Copyright © 2009 by the Hoover Institution. All rights reserved. Reproduced by permission.

The problem of underage drinking on college campuses has been brewing for many years to the continued vexation of higher education administrators. In 2008, John McCardell, president emeritus of Middlebury College, began to circulate for signature a public statement among colleagues titled "The Amethyst Initiative," which calls for elected officials to reexamine underage drinking laws. The project grew out of outreach efforts of a nonprofit organization he founded in 2007 called Choose Responsibility. The nonprofit advocates lowering the drinking age to 18 and licensing alcohol use for young people in much the same manner as driving—following coursework and an exam. Choose Responsibility also favors the repeal of the laws that set 21 as the mandatory minimum age for drinking (known as the "21 laws") and encourages states at the least to adopt exceptions to the 21 laws that would allow minors to drink at home and in private clubs. It also favors social changes that shift the focus on alcohol use among youth to the home, family, and individual.

"Rethinking" Twenty-One

The Amethyst Initiative's statement has been signed by 135 college presidents and chancellors at schools from Duke to Bennington. The majority is private; most are in the Northeast. The statement takes no formal position, unlike Choose Responsibility. It does, however, drop heavy hints as to where the debate ought to come out. The statement says "21 is not working" and asks "How many times must we relearn the lessons of Prohibition?" It draws comparisons to other age-of-majority rights conferred on 18-year-olds, such as voting and serving in the military, and calls upon elected officials to consider "whether current public policies are in line with current realities."

It seems that the presidents of 135 colleges, including elite schools, large universities, and small state schools find themselves so exasperated with the amount of alcohol guzzled by undergraduates—or more to the point, the trouble the undergraduates get into while inebriated—that they now beseech lawmakers to "rethink 21," an elegant and rather round-about way of saying: Let undergrads drink with the sanction of the law.

The primary argument made in the Initiative's statement in favor of repealing the 21 laws is that the 21 laws make alcohol taboo, thus driving underage drinking underground and causing more binge drinking to take place than otherwise would, due to the allure of forbidden fruit and the need for secrecy. Hence, by lowering the drinking age, youth consumption would come out in the open and binge drinking would be largely reduced or even eliminated. The second salutary effect of lowering the drinking age, the Initiative argues, would be educational: Colleges would be allowed to have open, frank discussions about responsible drinking. In other words, institutions of higher education could teach young people how to drink responsibly. The Initiative makes vague references to the "unintended consequences" of 21 "posing increasing risks to young people," and says that the original impetus for the 21 laws—reduction of highway fatalities by young drivers—has outlived its usefulness.

Since its launch, the Initiative has created a public dialog about the drinking age, resulting in media coverage and a hearing before the New Jersey state legislature in November 2008. Despite its gravity as a public health problem, even among children younger than 18, the topic of underage alcohol abuse has been underaddressed in the popular media and in public funding compared to illicit drug abuse. The Initiative is a welcome development insofar as it challenges us to examine whether 21 "is working." The answer. It is not, as currently enforced. So should 21 be scrapped or salvaged? . . .

Lowering the Legal Age Will Not Stop Binge Drinking

The logic of the Initiative is that if we take away the allure of illegality, American youth will stop binging. That conclusion is wrong. Alcohol should be forbidden to 18- to 20-year-olds

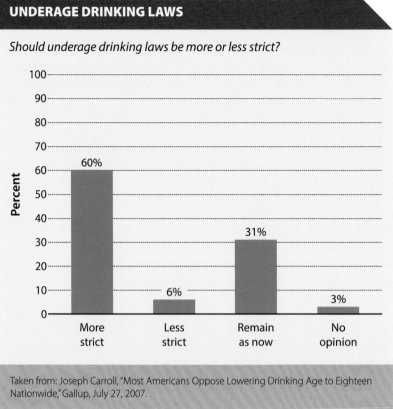

MOST AMERICANS OPPOSE ANY RELAXATION OF UNDERAGE DRINKING LAWS

Should underage drinking laws be more or less strict?

Taken from: Joseph Carroll, "Most Americans Oppose Lowering Drinking Age to Eighteen Nationwide," Gallup, July 27, 2007.

precisely because *they have a propensity* to binge drink whether the stuff is illegal or not—especially males.

Henry Wechsler and Toben F. Nelson, in the landmark Harvard School of Public Health College Alcohol Study, or CAS, which tracked college student drinking patterns from 1992 to 2001, explained that binge drinking is five or more drinks on one occasion. Binge drinking brings the blood alcohol concentration to 0.08 gram percent or above (typically five drinks for a man or four for a woman within two hours). To understand just how drunk that makes a person, consider that it violates criminal laws to drive with a blood alcohol level of 0.08 gram percent or above.

To call alcohol taboo implies that drinking is done in secret and rarely. Yet college drinking is so common as to have lost all tinge of intrigue. Drinking greases the social wheels, and college life for many is saturated with popular drinking games that no doubt seem brilliant to the late-adolescent: Beerchesi, Beergammon, BeerSoftball, coin games like Psycho, Quarters, and BeerBattleship, and card and dice games linked to beer.

When undergraduates binge drink, they get into trouble—a lot of it. They endanger and sometimes kill their fellow students by setting fires. They sexually assault their female companions (approximately 100,000 incidents annually). They get into fights with other young undergrads (some 700,000 assaults annually). On average 1,100 a year die from alcohol-related traffic crashes and another 300 die in nontraffic alcohol-related deaths. According to the CAS, among the 8 million college students in the United States surveyed in one study year, more than 2 million drove under the influence of alcohol and more than 3 million rode in cars with drivers who had been drinking. Eight percent of students—474,000—have unprotected consensual sex each year because they have been drinking. In short, college students do stupid, illegal, dangerous, and sometimes deadly things when they drink.

Moreover, the drinking doesn't begin in college. More kids drink alcohol than smoke pot, which is the most commonly used illicit drug. A third of our youth taste their first drink before the age of 13 and have drinking patterns as early as 8th to 10th grade. In a pattern that continues in college, boys fall into binge drinking patterns in greater numbers than girls by 12th grade. The Pacific Institute for Research and Evaluation has estimated the social cost of underage drinking (for all youth) at some $53 billion. That includes only highway deaths and injuries and does not factor in brain damage associated with early adolescent drinking, or the array of other injuries and social problems such as opportunity costs that crop up when children drink.

The majority of those who binge drink in college started down that road long before they matriculated—they simply continue their drinking habits once they arrive on campus. Brett Sokolow, president of the consulting firm National Center for Higher Education Risk Management (NCHERM), which counsels colleges on reducing "risk" through educational programs and institutional policies, said in an interview that based on his anecdotal experience, 60 to 70 percent of the students attending his on-campus alcohol seminars have had drinking experiences prior to attending college and about 40 percent have "deeply engrained drinking habits" by the time they get to college.

Consider the scope of college drinking. Among the general population in America, 15 percent of 18- to 25-year-olds binge drink, according to the Centers for Disease Control. Among college students, 80 percent reported drinking and of those, 40 percent binge drink once a month—that is more than twice the rate of their peers in the general population. About one fourth drank in this way frequently—three or more times in a two week period.

If college life, with its basic structure and lack of privacy, forces drinking underground as the Amethyst Initiative posits, then one should see far less binge drinking among youth who are not in college. A study drawn on data from the National Household Survey on Drug Abuse, which looked at heavy episodic drinking among all 18- to 24-year-olds, comparing those in college to those outside the ivy-covered walls, does not bear out the Initiative's theory. While 41 percent of those in college binge drank at least once a month, according to that study, so did 36 percent of other youth. . . .

Comparing Other Settings

Other settings bear comparison. American students studying abroad in France or Italy notice that college students there don't drink like fish, and assume that is the case among young people everywhere in Europe. While many Americans cling to the belief that Europeans are better than us, studies of drinking habits across all of Europe show that their binge drinking problems are worse than ours in many countries, start at younger ages, and continue into adulthood.

The legal drinking ages in Europe generally range from 16 to 18 with varying rules as to when youth may purchase and consume alcohol. Serious binge drinking begins at age 15 in countries across the European Union. The highest rates are seen in the Nordic countries, Slovenia, Latvia, the UK, and Ireland. Young teenagers, 15- to 16-year-olds, are drinking six drinks at a clip when they go out (even more in the UK and Ireland), and 18 percent of that age group is binge drinking three times a month. Things aren't much better south of the equator. When New Zealand lowered its drinking age to 18 it experienced a "sharp increase in binge drinking among teenagers and young adults." . . .

Alcohol Consumption Is Different from Other Age-of-Majority Rights

The Initiative takes pains to refer to college students as "adults," and argues that the 21 laws should be brought "into sync" with age-of-majority rights such as voting, military service, or contract. These are not apt comparisons because the basis of those rights is the doctrine of emancipation. Given the grave consequences of underage alcohol consumption, the legal test for emancipation is helpful in thinking about whether the typical American 18-year-old is mature enough for the rights and responsibilities of legal drinking.

When a minor enters the military (with parental permission), he or she *automatically* becomes emancipated in the eyes of the law. The law assumes that the military will only accept someone who demonstrates the necessary level of maturity for duty. In the event the military is wrong, it has an excellent system for weeding out mistakes: basic training. The military can discharge those not up to the challenge. For a minor to become emancipated under other circumstances, it's a tougher process. He must show a court that he is self-supporting, can handle his own personal affairs, and understands what emancipation means.

Although a typical 18-year-old is technically emancipated, it is the rare college student who could pass such a test. Rather than living a life of real emancipation like his married or enlisted counterparts, the college student exists in a strange netherworld suspended between adolescence and real adulthood. While college students demonstrate a good deal of independence in the sense that they live away from home, make friends, study, and do their own laundry, they are nonetheless dependent on their parents financially and demonstrate varying degrees of autonomy and good sense. They are often busy having the time of their lives. Indeed, a common suggestion for reigning in campus drinking is to hold classes on Friday mornings, thus preventing the weekend revelry from beginning on Thursday nights.

Alcohol consumption is unique among the rights conferred by age-of-majority laws because it alters brain chemistry, and the risk of conferring it on the wrong person can be immediate and violent. Bear in mind that under various provisions of state and federal law, even minors emancipated at an early age through marriage or military service see no change in their right to drink.

In addition, colleges are not the bastions of the hale and hearty they were for most of the 20th century. Today, students attend college while managing chronic illnesses such as arthritis, diabetes, multiple sclerosis, asthma, depression and other psychiatric maladies, endocrine disorders, and attention deficit disorder. College populations even include cancer survivors in various stages of remission. "Two generations ago [ill students] would not have been mainstreamed," said Patricia Fennell, head of Albany Health Management Associates and an expert on managing chronic health conditions. Now they are coping with chronic illnesses far from the watchful eyes of their parents—which means taking medicines and dealing with the temptations of college life—including alcohol.

Opponents of lowering the drinking age say that binge drinking is a problem among young people and that removing barriers to purchasing alcohol would only increase the problem. © Chuck Savage/Corbis.

Emancipation is not always desirable. Indeed, there is a tradition in the law to that effect. Many states have an express, statutory exception to age-of-majority emancipation rules. Exceptions usually relate to special rights conferred on the disabled, who are entitled to certain protections beyond the age of 18. Many state and federal child poverty programs cover children through age 21. Given the rates of binge drinking on campus and the number of deaths, injuries, and social costs associated with underage alcohol use, the emancipation-exception doctrines provide a useful perspective from which to think about the 21 laws. By delaying legal drinking, the 21 laws provide a valuable, *partial* exception to emancipation for 18-, 19- and 20-year-olds on the grounds that when it comes to alcohol, they can benefit from society's protection. . . .

Why Not Just Educate?

Choose Responsibility would replace the 21 laws with alcohol education at home and on campus. But colleges already educate college students about drinking. Even though schools are required to have anti-underage drinking policies under federal law, there is nothing to prevent them from teaching moderation or techniques to prevent alcohol poisoning. Indeed, college students get alcohol education from numerous sources: official school policy and abstinence programs and alcohol moderation programs provided by colleges; moderation programs provided by outside consulting groups; an online program called AlcoholEdu that has reached almost a quarter of a million students on over 400 college campuses; and normative marketing programs. Sokolow estimates that 10 to 20 percent of colleges now have outside consultants come to campus to provide alcohol moderation programs.

A large role is also played by social-norms marketing programs in which "latent healthy norms" about college drinking are made known to students through posters, flyers, and other forms of high-profile communication on campus. In other words, messages on billboards and flyers all over campus model the way grown-ups drink. A program may present the idea that a typical young drinker consumes *five or fewer* drinks when he parties with friends. Such marketing programs carry a positive message and do *not* discuss the dangers of drinking. About half of all four-year residential colleges have conducted social-norms marketing programs for alcohol.

They are not necessarily a good idea. A study of alcohol-related social-norms marketing was done based on the data gathered in the Harvard CAS that compared the 118 schools in the survey. The social-norms study included the schools that had experienced social-norms marketing programs and those that didn't. The study showed that social-norms marketing did not reduce college drinking. In fact, in the schools that had the programs, drinking increased. In the schools without the programs, no change in drinking rates occurred.

The study did not show why drinking increased at schools with the programs, but it is a cautionary tale. The college drinking scene is a battleground with two fronts: coping with those who already are binge drinkers and fighting for the hearts and souls of the others. We know that about half of freshman classes enter with no history of alcohol use and can be lured into drinking. Hearing a message sanctioned by the college that some drinking is all right could tip the balance.

We do know that many environmental factors influence the likelihood of a nondrinking student continuing on that course, including diversity of the student body, the number of female students, the risk and cost of obtaining alcohol and the presence of "zero-tolerance" dorms. Much depends on the state and its culture of enforcement. Measures such as increasing prices, imposing excise taxes, and local laws that regulate the density of liquor-selling establishments close to campus can have a strong impact on underage drinking.

The Institute of Alcohol Studies in London looked at individual as well as meta-analyses of European, Australian, and

American youth alcohol education efforts. It found that although there were "individual examples of the beneficial impacts of school-based education," there was not enough evidence to conclude that education has an impact on binge drinking among young people. The Institute said it was not implying that education should not be done, but it "should not be seen as the answer to reduce the harm done by binge drinking." Education, the Institute concluded, plays only a supportive role.

A Big, Untested Assumption

The Amethyst Initiative says, in essence, that the phenomenon of underage drinking is a tidal wave that society cannot stop. Our only hope is to ride the wave along with our children, give them an oar, and hope they don't drown. That relies on the very big—and untested—assumption that their young minds have the capacity to listen when it comes to alcohol, no matter how badly they want to party, hook up, fit in.

Given the stakes, America should not throw in the towel on the 21 laws until we have actually enforced them as they were meant to be enforced—though it will require a clear dedication of political will. It can be done; a similar revolution occurred during the 1980s with respect to driving under the influence laws. Disparities in enforcement do not mean that the laws are impossible to enforce. It signals that we have not gotten serious as a nation about using the laws we have—and improving them where needed.

"The practice of using routine Breath-alyzers (all students breathalyzed at all dances) is the most suitable option to deter drinking at school dances."

Alcohol Screening at High School Dances Should Be Mandatory

The Fairfield Ludlowe High School Parent Teacher Association

In the following viewpoint, the Fairfield Ludlowe High School Parent Teacher Association (PTA) supports the routine use of breathalyzers at high school dances to screen for student drinking. According to the PTA, most alcohol-related school suspensions occur at these events, and extensive research and experience at other high schools demonstrate that breathalyzers effectively deter student alcohol use without raising issues of liability or constitutionality. However, the PTA committee indicates that Fairfield's Board of Education has been slow to adopt an alcohol-screening policy despite the urgent risks of drinking at dances and proms. Fairfield Ludlowe High School is located in Fairfield, Connecticut.

The 2009–2010 Executive Board and Committee Chairmen, Fairfield Ludlowe High School Parent Teacher Association, "Opinion: The Case for Prom Breathalyzers," *Fairfield Citizen*, May 28, 2010. Copyright © 2010 by the Fairfield Citizen. All rights reserved. Reproduced by permission.

Both Fairfield Ludlowe and Fairfield Warde high school administrators have asked the Board of Education to create a policy that authorizes them to use Breathalyzers at all high school dance attendees. The decision to request this policy did not come easily, nor was it hastily made. It has surely evolved from years of collective experience as dance chaperones and observing firsthand the realities of the times. Our administrators state that nearly all of our alcohol-related high school suspensions occur at dances.

Realizing the challenges that our administrators have faced in order to protect the wellness and safety of all students at dances, a Joint High School PTA [Parent Teacher Association] Task Force offered to research this issue in October 2008. Their year-long research included meeting with educational professionals, inquiring to neighboring districts, attending related events in similar communities, analyzing student surveys and interviewing staff, students and parents. They Googled, e-mailed, queried and consulted both locally and nationally. Their sources have included other Fairfield County high schools, the Fairfield Police Department, the first selectman's Task Force on Alcohol and Health, Trumbull Partnership Against Underage Drinking, Connecticut Association of Boards of Education, drug/alcohol counselors (both at our high schools and privately practicing), attorneys, pediatric neurologists, alcohol detection device manufacturers, Gov. M. Jodi Rell's office and even the United States Supreme Court.

The Most Suitable Option

After their extensive research, the PTA committee conferred with administrators and concluded that the practice of using routine Breathalyzers (all students breathalyzed at all dances) is the most suitable option to deter drinking at school dances. Questions of liability, effectiveness, Fourth Amendment (search and seizure) rights, practicality and expense were all quelled by their research findings and the testimony of administrators

Many school districts and high school students across the United States feel that alcohol consumption at prom is a large problem. © Jupiterimages/Getty Images.

at Greenwich, Darien, New Canaan, Ridgefield, Wilton and Trumbull High Schools where Breathalyzers have been administered routinely at all dances for several years now. All of these high schools report extremely high satisfaction with their routine Breathalyzer policy. Many emphasized the ease of use and accuracy of the passive (no contact with mouth) devices, the quick acceptance by students and, most importantly, the tremendous reduction in alcohol-related incidents. In fact, Greenwich High reports no positive test results at any dance in the past four years. Furthermore, no school has reported any legal challenges resulting from this policy.

"The kids know they will stop, blow and go at every dance and they know we want them to be safe," says Kathy Steiner, a Greenwich High School wellness teacher. "The intention of this policy is not to 'catch' students drinking, rather, it is to give them a very good reason not to drink before or during prom. It works. The stakes are too high to not protect our children this way."

The committee presented its findings and BOE [board of education] policy recommendation to the 2009–10 Fairfield PTA Council where it was supported unanimously by all 16 Fairfield PTA presidents. Then, last Oct. 26 [2009], a full year since they initiated the research, they culminated their efforts with a presentation at a Joint High School PTA Task Force meeting which included this motion:

> For reasons of absolute equity, consistency and objectivity, and to effectively deter students from drinking as well as to protect the wellness and safety of ALL students at our dances, we hereby request that our Board of Education members create a policy which makes routine the use of Breathalyzers at our high school dances and to take all action required to affect this change at our spring 2010 dances.

This motion was passed unanimously. . . .

Putting Our Children at Risk

It is now 7 months later and most of our 2010 proms have come and gone. Shockingly, there still exists no Fairfield Board of Education policy on using Breathalyzers. A series of missteps have occurred since the Board of Education took this issue under consideration. To her credit, Chairman Sue Brand encouraged the BOE Sub-Committee on Policy (chaired by Stacey Zahn) to develop a Breathalyzer policy early this year.

Apparently, half a year was not enough time to formulate a policy of one or two simple sentences that would direct the administrators to "use Breathalyzers on all students at all dances." Zahn submitted a disjointed paragraph as policy at the March 9 [2010] BOE meeting that lacked clarity and authority. A bewildered-looking full board recommended to return it to the Policy Sub-committee for revisions.

Incredibly, the second version proposed at the April 27 BOE meeting was nearly identical and included language that continued to dissatisfy most members. Knowing time was now of the essence and determined to insure a safe and healthy 2010 prom season, [Perry] Liu motioned to amend its wording at the table in hopes of salvaging a simple and direct policy that could be voted on that night as the agenda had stated. Although [Catherine] Albin abstained, the majority agreed to approve Liu's changes in wording.

But the pre-vote discussion revealed a more serious road-block than ambiguous vocabulary. While listening to the BOE members openly discuss Breathalyzers, our proms, past practice, underage drinking and the law, it became apparent that many of them had not done their homework. Their comments often indicated a lack of research and knowledge of the issue. This was particularly frustrating for parents and staff in the audience who were well-versed on this important issue but had never been contacted for their research.

Perhaps confusing lack of understanding for controversy, Albin suddenly moved to table the policy vote and the new vote date became June 8—well after the 2010 proms. This appeared to many to be an attempt to avoid taking a stand on a timely and critical issue affecting the health and safety of our children. [Pam] Iacono apologized for the delay but stated that "it all felt too rushed." Too rushed? Nine people had seven months to write a two-sentence policy that most of our neighboring schools have been successfully implementing for many years. All the while, the BOE's Policy Sub-committee was just a phone call away from accessing a year's worth of relevant research compiled by educational advocates in our own community.

We thank Brand, Liu and Sue Dow for their supportive words and votes to courageously attempt to provide the routine Breathalyzer policy this year to assist our high school administrators in creating a safer setting for our proms.

We also must directly state our disappointment in the rest of the BOE members for having failed to respect the timeline to keep safe and healthy the more than 1,500 Fairfield teenagers who will have attended our 2010 proms. Regrettably, we see

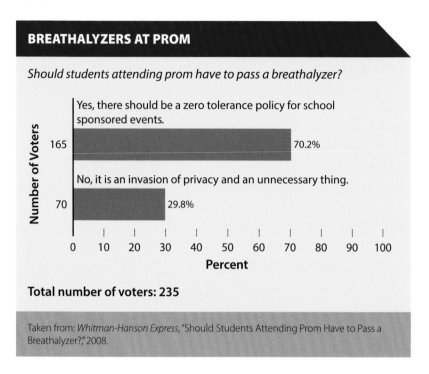

BREATHALYZERS AT PROM

Should students attending prom have to pass a breathalyzer?

Number of Voters

Yes, there should be a zero tolerance policy for school sponsored events.

165 � bar▮ 70.2%

No, it is an invasion of privacy and an unnecessary thing.

70 ▮ 29.8%

Percent: 0 10 20 30 40 50 60 70 80 90 100

Total number of voters: 235

Taken from: *Whitman-Hanson Express*, "Should Students Attending Prom Have to Pass a Breathalyzer?," 2008.

no evidence of any sense of urgency or priority in regard to a Breathalyzer policy or, for that matter, any initiative to address the troubling underage drinking issues presented in the 2008 RYASAP [Regional Youth Adult Social Action Partnership] report which they all received more than 18 months ago. Their lack of focus, decisiveness and action is unacceptable. They have put our children's well being at risk.

15

VIEWPOINT

"The mandatory breathalyzer test requirement for prom can infringe on the constitutional rights of the high school students."

Mandatory Alcohol Screening at High School Proms Raises Constitutional Concerns

Jonathan Motto

In the following viewpoint, Jonathan Motto contends that mandatory alcohol screening with breathalyzers at high school proms raises a variety of constitutional concerns. He states that required breathalyzer testing may intrude on privacy, impose school restrictions in off-campus locations, introduce unreasonable police enforcement, restrict the rights of adult students, and discourage prom attendance among those unwilling to be tested. The dangers of underage drinking and driving, Motto observes, will likely outweigh the possible constitutional infringements in the courts. However, he advises that considerations and measures should be

Jonathan Motto, "The Newest Prom Accessory: Breathalyzer Tests: A Discussion of the Fourth Amendment Implications Raised by Mandatory Breathalyzer Tests at Prom," Loyola University Chicago School of Law, Child Law and Education Institute, May 18, 2011, pp. 1–2, 5–14.

taken in breathalyzer testing to balance students' rights and safety. Motto is an associate attorney at McDermott Will and Emery in Chicago, Illinois.

It's that time of year again. The time when the weather gets warm, the flowers begin to bloom, and high school students anxiously await their prom. Shopping malls are littered with brightly colored dresses, nail salons and hair dressers are booked through the month of May, and tuxedo rental companies are constantly explaining the difference between a bow tie and a regular tie to high school boys. But prom is not just about the fancy clothes, the nice hair, the limousines, or the flowers; it is also closely associated with spiked-punch bowls, pre- and post-prom parties that serve alcohol, and unfortunately an increase in drunk driving accidents. The prevalence of underage drinking at prom has prompted community groups, such as Mothers Against Drunk Driving and Students Against Destructive Decisions, to set up presentations, demonstrations, television commercials, and other awareness campaigns to help curb the presence of alcohol at prom.

While schools have traditionally followed suit with school assemblies discussing the dangers of drinking and live demonstrations of drunk driving accidents, high school boards and administrators have recently used a new approach: breathalyzer tests. Schools across the country now require attendees to take a breathalyzer test before being admitted to prom. While the intent of this procedure is clearly to prevent drinking before prom, some question whether it goes too far. A number of parents and organizations have been outspoken against breathalyzer tests at prom because, they argue, these tests violate the student's Fourth Amendment rights to be free from unreasonable search and seizure. With the danger of alcohol use at prom and the likelihood of drunk driving accidents as a result, are the students truly being denied their constitutional rights by these new policies? . . .

Breathalyzer Tests Raise Constitutional Concerns

Some parents and activist groups have been outspoken against school policies that require students to submit to a breathalyzer test before entering the prom. . . . It seems fairly clear from the case law that requiring students who exhibit signs of intoxication to submit to a breathalyzer would fall within the reasonableness standard upheld by the Court in [*New Jersey v.*] *T.L.O.* As such, the concerns discussed below focus mainly on the requirement that *all* students attending prom submit to a breathalyzer test even if they are not exhibiting signs of intoxication.

Nature of Breathalyzer Test. Most mandatory breathalyzer test policies require students to take the breathalyzer test when they are in line, waiting to enter the prom. The test is given to each student while others wait in line for their turn. Picture a line of big dresses, tuxedos, tiaras, and flowers all shuffling along waiting to blow into a breathalyzer machine. The nature of the breathalyzer makes each student submit to the test in front of their peers, who will all then be aware of the results of the test. The nature of the breathalyzer test intrudes on the student's privacy because the test is conducted in the presence of other students and the results are known to a larger number of people (both school officials and students).

Location of Prom. For many high schools, prom is located in a hotel ballroom, museum, or other private venue not on school property. While prom is still a school-sponsored event, students can choose to attend or not attend, and usually pay for a ticket and take their own transportation to and from the event. In this instance, do the restrictions imposed on students' Fourth Amendment rights behind the "school gates" apply when the student is outside the physical gates but still at a school function? Because prom is beyond the physical premises of the school, some may argue the constitutional restrictions imposed

Dispelling the Myth of the Heavy Teen Drinker

Graduation and prom season usually bring a flurry of concern about underage drinking. A May 2005 *Denver Post* story, "Graduation Celebrations often Leave Teens at Risk," noted that "teens too often confuse celebration with intoxication," and that "teens who drink are more likely to commit or be the victim of violence." These statements may be true, but they are certainly not only true for teens. . . . Results from the 2003 National Survey on Drug Use and Health (NSDUH) indicate that heavy drinking is highest for twenty-one- to twenty-five-year-olds. For those under eighteen, adults outdo them in heavy drinking until age fifty.

> *Karen Sternheimer,* Kids These Days: Facts and Fictions About Today's Youth. *Lanham, MD: Rowman & Littlefield, 2006.*

on students no longer apply or no longer apply to the same degree.

Personnel Administering the Breathalyzer Test. Generally, schools have administrators, teachers, or other chaperones administer the breathalyzer test as students enter the prom. In this case, the reasoning of the Supreme Court . . . applies to the tests given by school personnel. The issue becomes a greater constitutional infringement if police officers or other law enforcement personnel administer the breathalyzer test. Now, there are shuffling dresses and tuxedos blowing into a breathalyzer machine operated by a police officer, possibly in uniform. Some may argue this is unreasonable given the intent of the policy to prevent drinking before prom. The possible criminal and legal ramifications associated with involving law enforcement officials in breathalyzer testing at prom may be a greater infringement on the students' rights that outweighs the need for such a policy.

High School Seniors. Prom is usually for high school junior and seniors. In many cases, high school seniors have turned eighteen by the time prom occurs. If a student has reached the age of majority, he or she is no longer subject to the restricted constitutional freedoms associated with minority. Now that these students are viewed as adults in the eyes of the law, are able to vote, and can serve in the military, some believe these students should not face the same restrictions in their Fourth Amendment rights as other minor students.

Voluntary Attendance at Prom. While it is true that students decide whether to attend prom and are not forced by the school to go, is prom really voluntary? In *Santa Fe Independent School District v. Jane Doe*, the Court held high school football games were not completely voluntary because some students had to attend them for extracurricular activities or class credit and the social pressure of being in high school made it difficult for students not to attend. Prom, even more so than football games, is an iconic moment in high school that is built-up throughout the entire school year. Not only is there food, music, and dancing with friends, but also prom themes, prom songs, and even a king and queen. Similar to the reasoning employed in *Santa Fe*, requiring students to submit to a breathalyzer may prevent students, who do not wish to submit to a breathalyzer test, from attending their high school prom.

Alcohol Abuse and Drunk Driving Prevention. As a final consideration, the intent of the policy is to prevent drinking before prom and reduce the number of alcohol-related accidents involving high school students, but does the policy actually accomplish this goal? Instead of attending prom, those that wish to drink may do so in unsafe environments, exposing themselves and others to greater risk. Additionally, if a student comes to prom and tests positive for alcohol, what happens to that student? Is he or she sent home? What if they drove to prom, do they drive home? There are various additional considerations that must accompany the breathalyzer test policy for it to actually have its intended effect. Without these additional steps, it may only make the problem worse.

Despite the concerns and constitutional infringements highlighted above, it seems that mandatory breathalyzer tests before entering prom will be held constitutional by the courts. After examining the policy and its intent, it is likely a court will find the special needs exception is also present in this case. To understand this position, this Section applies the Court's balancing test outlined in *T.L.O.* and subsequent cases to a mandatory breathalyzer test policy for admission to prom.

Expectation of Privacy

The first factor in the balancing test examined by the Court is the "nature of the private interest upon which the search . . . at issue intrudes." While the Court recognizes that children lack some of the most fundamental rights of self-determination, *Tinker [v. Des Moines School District]* demonstrates students do not give up all of their constitutional liberties when they go school. Therefore, high school students do have an expectation of privacy even at school. In the case of prom, students may even have a higher expectation of privacy because they are usually no longer on school property. Additionally, the student or the student's date purchased the ticket, making it seem that prom is a private event. As such, students have a heightened expectation of privacy at prom compared to their expectation of privacy when attending class on a routine basis at the school.

The Court has consistently held, however, the Fourth Amendment does not protect all subjective expectations of privacy, but rather, only those expectations which society recognizes as "legitimate." While the reasonableness standard set forth in *T.L.O.* does little to shed light on the constitutional question raised by mandatory, suspicion-less breathalyzer testing, the Court's reasoning in *Vernonia* [*School District v. Acton*] indicates that the students' legitimate expectations of privacy are actually less than they might think. Despite the argument that prom is a "rite of passage" and social pressure requires students to attend, prom is very much a voluntary event.

Prom tickets must be paid for by students, there is usually no school requirement to attend prom, prom is not a mandatory part of high school that must be completed before graduation, and a number of students do not attend prom each year. At almost any school, prom is completely voluntary. By purchasing the ticket, students agree to subject themselves to the additional regulations and restrictions imposed by the school. These additional regulations may include what the student can wear, who the student can bring as a date, where the student can go after prom, and now what tests the student must perform to get in to the event. As reasoned in *Vernonia*, students who voluntarily participate in an activity have "reason to expect intrusions upon normal rights and privileges, including privacy." Therefore, a court will likely determine that students have a reduced legitimate expectation of privacy by choosing to attend prom.

This line of reasoning is even stronger when students are afforded notice of the additional requirements. If students are aware, prior to deciding to attend prom, that they will be forced to take a breathalyzer test to get into the event, their legitimate expectation of privacy is further reduced when they still decide to attend. Many schools post the regulations (including the mandatory breathalyzer test) on prom flyers throughout the school, print them on prom tickets, or even announce them at a meeting for students and their parents. With advanced notice, a student's legitimate expectation of privacy is made even less than that of student athletes or members of competitive student organizations. Therefore, a court is even more likely to determine that students have a reduced legitimate expectation of privacy when it comes to attending prom.

Level of Intrusiveness

Under the balancing test, the students' legitimate expectation of privacy is weighed against the level of intrusiveness of the search. While blowing on a breathalyzer machine is not an "excretory function" in the same sense as a urine drug test, a breathalyzer test may still be intrusive. Testing a person's breath is a very close encounter and can be considered highly intrusive because the "body and its odors are highly personal." In both *Vernonia* and [*Board of Education v.*] *Earls*, however, the Court held a student urine test conducted partially in front of school officials was not highly intrusive so as to make the policy unconstitutional. For the breathalyzer test, students remain fully clothed, are not in a traditionally private place (such as a bathroom), and are not performing an excretory function in front of school officials. Given the nature of the breathalyzer test, it seems unlikely a court will deem it overly intrusive.

However, in both *Vernonia* and *Earls*, the Court relied on the fact that the results of the drug test would be used for a narrow purpose of determining athletic eligibility and only a limited number of school officials would receive the results. The breathalyzer test is conducted outside the prom venue, in front of the other students waiting to take the test, and in the presence of school officials. The results of the test are immediately known to anyone and everyone at prom. Even if other students do not see a student taking the test, they will know if another student tested positive for alcohol consumption by word of mouth and the simple fact the student did not enter the event. If a police officer administers the test or if the results are given to law enforcement officials, this may create additional intrusion issues that should be considered by a court. However, because the breathalyzer test only provides results on alcohol consumption, the same concerns of medical history and disease disclosure present with drug testing are not an issue in this case. As such, it is likely a court will find the level of intrusiveness of a breathalyzer test relatively low despite the concerns raised above.

Members of Students Against Drunk Driving of Independence High School in Ohio stage a mock car crash to warn fellow students not to drink and drive during prom in 2007. As an alternative to alcohol screenings, some schools use educational programs like this one to discourage drinking at prom. © AP Images/The Plain Dealer, John Kuntz.

Nature and Immediacy of the Government's Concern

The final factor of the balancing test examines the nature and immediacy of the governmental concern at issue. No one will argue deterring underage drinking is not an important concern that should be addressed by the government. According to a 2009 study by the National Institute of Drug Use, nearly three-quarters of students (72%) have consumed alcohol by the end of high school and more than a third (37%) have done so by eighth grade. Alcohol consumption is the cause of 60% of all teen deaths involving car accidents, with the number of accidents increasing around prom season. With staggering statistics like these, the nature and immediacy factor of preventing underage drinking at prom will be met. Given underage drinking is a national problem, even preventative policies aimed at deterring alcohol consumption by high school students will pass the nature and immediacy test at all high schools. Therefore, a high school does not have to wait for a demonstrated alcohol consumption problem among its students, but rather, it can require breathalyzer tests at prom given the nature and immediacy of the national underage drinking problem.

Balancing the Factors

To summarize, high school students attending prom have a relatively low legitimate expectation of privacy at prom, especially if given notice. Additionally, a breathalyzer test is fairly unobtrusive given the other school policies the Court has recognized as unobtrusive. These two concerns create a small infringement on a high school student's Fourth Amendment right to be free from unreasonable search and seizure. This small infringement will likely be outweighed by the great need to deter high school students from engaging in underage drinking. As such, a school policy requiring mandatory breathalyzer tests to enter prom will likely withstand a constitutional challenge given the current decisions of the Supreme Court.

Recommendations for Instituting a Mandatory Breathalyzer Test Policy for Prom

In 2002, the Office of Drug Control Policy published a guide for schools to decide whether and how to conduct drug tests of their students. In adopting a similar approach, this Section of the [viewpoint] provides recommendations for high schools considering whether and how to implement a mandatory breathalyzer test requirement for prom.

- First, schools should determine there is a need for this policy by considering the underage drinking problem in the school and surrounding school districts. Then, the school should consider alternative policies also aimed at reducing underage drinking to determine if mandatory breathalyzer tests at prom are the best option.

- Having decided to adopt a breathalyzer requirement for prom, schools need to decide the type of policy and test to be administered, who should administer it, where the test takes place, the consequences of the test, the procedure for a student that is found to have consumed alcohol, etc. School districts will differ in the specifications of their respective policies. Schools need to consider what policies work best for their students and for reducing underage drinking in their community. The less intrusive the policy, the more likely it will be accepted by students and parents and pass a constitutional challenge.

- Each of the decisions described in the previous recommendation should be a product of discussions and research conducted by the school board, school administrators, teachers, counselors, parents, and the community. Only by involving each of these parties can a school create support for the policy and explain the reasons and goals of instituting such a policy.

- Once the parameters of the policy are decided, students and parents should be notified of the policy prior to making the decision to attend prom. This can be done by posting prom rules and regulations throughout the school in the weeks leading up to prom, giving students a handout with this information before they purchase their tickets, putting the information on the back of the prom ticket, and by telling parents and students at a mandatory meeting for those wishing to attend prom.

- At the event, schools should adhere to the policy that was implemented and disclosed to the students and their parents. The test results should be given to as few school officials as possible and not disclosed to other students or the community.

The mandatory breathalyzer test requirement for prom can infringe on the constitutional rights of the high school students. As such, school districts should take care in creating these policies to ensure the students' rights are protected as much as possible while also working to reduce the prevalence of underage drinking around prom.

Organizations to Contact

The editors have compiled the following list of organizations concerned with the issues debated in this book. The descriptions are derived from materials provided by the organizations. All have publications or information available for interested readers. The list was compiled on the date of publication of the present volume; the information provided here may change. Be aware that many organizations take several weeks or longer to respond to inquiries, so allow as much time as possible.

A Matter of Degree (AMOD)

401 Park Drive
Boston, MA 02215
e-mail: amod@hsph.harvard.edu
website: www.hsph.harvard.edu/amod

AMOD was developed by the Robert Wood Johnson Foundation to "bring campuses and communities together to change the conditions that promote heavy alcohol consumption prevalent in many campus-community environments." Ten campuses, ranging from the University of Delaware to the University of Wisconsin, have developed their own coalitions and programs using the task force's resources. The participating universities must demonstrate a coordinated effort with both the college campus and the surrounding community to discourage heavy alcohol consumption among college students.

Al-Anon/Alateen

1600 Corporate Landing Parkway
Virginia Beach, VA 23454
(757) 563-1600 • fax: (757) 563-1655
e-mail: wso@al-anon.org
website: www.al-anon.alateen.org

Al-Anon (which includes Alateen for younger members) has been offering support for friends and families of problem drinkers for more than half a century. The organization offers support meetings, based on a twelve-step model, around the country. On its website, users can find local meetings and order any of the organization's numerous publications, which include daily meditations and more comprehensive print resources for adults and teens coping with a loved one's alcoholism.

Alcohol Justice

24 Belvedere Street
San Rafael, CA 94901
(415) 456-5692
website: www.alcoholjustice.org

Formerly named the Marin Institute, Alcohol Justice is a watchdog group that monitors the alcohol industry's products and educates families and communities on ways to combat what it views as the industry's harmful influence. Current campaigns include banning so-called alcopops (sugary alcoholic beverages) and alcoholic energy drinks, increasing alcohol taxes, and regulating alcohol-advertising billboards. The institute's website outlines the alcohol industry's marketing tactics and offers numerous fact sheets on such topics. It also provides youth leaders and community organizers with resources to aid them in their work.

Amethyst Initiative

10 E Street, SE
Washington, DC 20003
(202) 543-8760 • fax: (202) 543-8764

Launched in July 2008 by Choose Responsibility, the Amethyst Initiative is made up of chancellors and presidents of universities and colleges across the United States. These higher education leaders have signed their names to a public statement asserting that the problem of irresponsible drinking by young people continues despite the minimum legal drinking age of twenty-one, and there is a culture of dangerous binge drinking on many campuses. The Amethyst Initiative supports informed and unimpeded debate on the legal drinking age of twenty-one.

Center on Alcohol Marketing and Youth (CAMY)
Johns Hopkins Bloomberg School of Public Health
624 N. Broadway, Suite 292
Baltimore, MD 21205
website: www.camy.org

CAMY was founded to monitor how the alcohol industry marketed its products to young people, culminating in a special report, "Youth Exposure to Alcohol Advertising on Television, 2001 to 2007." The CAMY site has a gallery of print and television ads for alcohol that support the center's conclusions about youth marketing and offers starting points for discussion. It also offers various fact sheets on topics related to underage drinking.

Choose Responsibility
PO Box 284
Ardsley on Hudson, NY 10503
(202) 543-8760 • fax: (202) 543-8764
e-mail: info@chooseresponsibility.org
website: www.chooseresponsibility.org

Founded by John M. McCardell Jr., president emeritus of Middlebury College, Choose Responsibility is a nonprofit organization that advocates lowering the minimum drinking age of twenty-one. It aims to stimulate informed and dispassionate public discussion about the presence of alcohol in US culture and encourages policies that will effectively empower young adults age eighteen to twenty to make mature decisions about the place of alcohol in their lives. The Choose Responsibility website details its proposal to lower the drinking age and provides a Frequently Asked Questions section, videos, and an online Volunteer Center.

Gordie Foundation

PO Box 800139
University of Virginia
Charlottesville, VA 22908-0139
(434) 924-5276 • fax: (434) 982-3671
e-mail: gordiecenter@virginia.edu
website: www.gordie.org

The Gordie Foundation was created in memory of Gordon Bailey, an eighteen-year-old freshman at the University of Colorado who died in 2004 of alcohol poisoning following a fraternity hazing ritual. The foundation's mission is "to provide today's young people with the skills to navigate the dangers of alcohol, binge drinking, peer pressure, and hazing." The Gordie Foundation offers several programs, which include public awareness campaigns, student education programs, and a movie highlighting the dangers of hazing.

Mothers Against Drunk Driving (MADD)

511 E. John Carpenter Freeway, Suite 700
Irving, TX 75062
(800) 438-6233 (ASK MADD) • fax: (972) 869-2206
website: www.madd.org

MADD was founded in 1980 by a mother whose young daughter was killed by a drunk driver. In addition to stopping drunk driving, the organization also actively works to discourage underage drinking. MADD works with lawmakers, advocating to keep the legal drinking age at twenty-one. Archived issues of the organization's newsletter, *MADDVOCATE*, are available online, as are fact sheets on grieving, injuries, legal and financial advice, and interventions.

SAM Spady Foundation

PO Box 701
Beatrice, NE 68310-0701
website: www.samspadyfoundation.org

The SAM (Student Alcohol Management) Spady Foundation was founded to honor the memory of Samantha Spady, who died of alcohol poisoning in 2004 at the age of nineteen. The foundation's mission is to "educate all parents and students on the dangers of alcohol, specifically high-risk consumption, and the signs and symptoms of alcohol poisoning." To that end, the foundation sponsors the formation of alcohol awareness and education programs on college and university campuses. It also has produced a DVD, *Death by Alcohol: The Sam Spady Foundation*, available for purchase on the website. Archived newsletter issues are also available for download.

For Further Reading

Books

David Aretha, *On the Rocks: Teens and Alcohol.* New York: Franklin Watts, 2007.

Richard J. Bonnie and Mary Ellen O'Connell, eds., *Reducing Underage Drinking: A Collective Responsibility.* Washington, DC: National Academies Press, 2004.

George W. Dowdall, *College Drinking: Reframing a Social Problem.* Westport, CN: Praeger, 2009.

Barron H. Lerner, *One for the Road: Drunk Driving Since 1900.* Baltimore, MD: Johns Hopkins University Press, 2011.

Daniel Okrent, *Last Call: The Rise and Fall of Prohibition.* New York: Scribner, 2010.

Garrett Peck, *The Prohibition Hangover: Alcohol in America from Demon Rum to Cult Cabernet.* New Brunswick, NJ: Rutgers University Press, 2009.

Barrett Seaman, *Binge: What Your College Student Won't Tell You.* Hoboken, NJ: John Wiley & Sons, 2005.

Christine Sismondo, *America Walks into a Bar: A Spirited History of Taverns and Saloons, Speakeasies, and Grog Shops.* New York: Oxford University Press, 2011.

Chris Volkmann and Toren Volkmann, *From Binge to Blackout: A Mother and Son Struggle with Teen Drinking.* New York: New American Library, 2006.

Koren Zailckas, *Smashed: Story of a Drunken Girlhood.* New York: Viking, 2005.

Periodicals and Internet Sources

Melinda Beck, "Dad, I Prefer the Shiraz," *Wall Street Journal,* March 8, 2011.

E. Chamberlain and R. Solomon, "Zero Blood Alcohol Concentration Limits for Drivers Under 21: Lessons from Canada," *Injury Prevention*, January 20, 2008.

Andrew Hitti, "The Drinking Age Is Stupid—and Unconstitutional," *Columbia Spectator*, September 17, 2009.

Leanne Italie, "Prom Season Puts the Spotlight on Underage Drinking Problem," *Huffington Post*, April 18, 2011.

John M. McCardell Jr., "Commentary: Drinking Age of 21 Doesn't Work," CNN.com, September 16, 2009.

Michelle Minton, "Lower the Drinking Age for Everyone," *National Review*, April 20, 2011.

Jeffrey A. Miron and Elina Tetelbaum, "The Dangers of the Drinking Age," *Forbes*, May 15, 2009.

Jessica Pauline Ogilvie, "Is Lowering the Drinking Age a Good Idea?," *Los Angeles Times*, May 30, 2011.

Veronika Oleksyn, "Kids in Europe Drinking Heavy at Early Age," *San Francisco Chronicle*, April 27, 2008.

Darshak Sanghavi, "Quicker Liquor," *Slate*, August 28, 2008.

Kirsten Scharnberg, "States Weighing Lower Age to Drink," *Chicago Times*, March 9, 2008.

Emma Schwartz, "A Host of Trouble," *US News & World Report*, September 29, 2007.

Fran Silverman, "A Different Kind of Student Exam," *New York Times*, March 30, 2008.

Christine Streed, "Teens, Alcohol, and Real Life," *Quintessential Barrington*, Spring 2008.

Scott Thill, "So Why, Exactly, Is the Drinking Age in the US Stuck at 21 Years?," *AlterNet*, July 6, 2011.

Index

US Secretary of Transportation, 12
US Supreme Court, 4–5, 9, 11–19,
    128
    See also specific cases

V
Vandalism, 94
Vermont, 4, 6–7, 54
Vernonia School District v. Acton,
    139–140
Victory, Jeffrey P., 31–38
Vietnam War, 4, 21, 53, 113
Violence, 94, 119, 136
Virginia, 46
Voting age, 4, 8, 113, 116, 137

W
Wakulich, Elizabeth, 5, 59
Wakulich, Mary Louise, 59
Wakulich v. Mraz (2003), 5–6, 10,
    58–68, 83, 86–87
Washington Post (newspaper),
    26–27
Wechsler, Henry, 118
Weicker, Lowell P., 24–25
Wells, H.G., 43
Wisconsin, 53

Z
Zahn, Stacey, 130